REPUBLIC'S A-10 THUNDERBOLT II

Also by Don Logan
ROCKWELL B-1B: SAC'S LAST BOMBER
NORTHROP'S T-38 TALON
NORTHROP'S YF-17 COBRA
THE 388TH TACTICAL FIGHTER WING AT KORAT RTAFB 1972

REPUBLIC'S A-10 THUNDERBOLT II

A Pictorial History
Don Logan

Schiffer Military History
Atglen, PA

ACKNOWLEDGEMENTS

I would like to thank the following individuals who have helped me in this project: Mr. C. John Amrhein of Northrop/Grumman Corporation, Gilles Auliard, Dana Bell, Tom Brewer, David F. Brown, Joe Bruch, Tim Doherty, Kevin Foy, Michael France, Alec Fushi, Jerry Geer, Jim Goodall, Norris Graser, Bob Greby, Paul Hart, Marty Isham, Renato E. F. Jones, Tom Kaminski, Craig Kaston, Ben Knowles, Ray Leader, Nate Leong, Jody Louviere, Patrick Martin, Charles Mayer, Don McGary, Hugh Muir, Kevin Patrick, Brian C. Rogers, Mick Roth, Tony Sacketos, Don Spering/AIR, Douglas Slowiak, Keith Snyder, Norm Taylor, Randy Walker, Pete Wilson, and Paul Withers. Thanks to the Public Affairs Offices of the A-10 units, especially the 917th Wing Barksdale AFB, LA. The unit flight suit patches were supplied by John Cook. Special thanks to Roger Johansen for the line art.

THE AUTHOR

After graduating from California State University-Northridge with a BA degree in History, Don Logan joined the USAF in August, 1969. He flew as an F-4E Weapon Systems Officer (WSO), stationed at Korat RTAFB in Thailand, flying 133 combat missions over North Vietnam, South Vietnam, and Laos before being shot down over North Vietnam on July 5, 1972. He spent nine months as a POW in Hanoi, North Vietnam. As a result of missions flown in Southeast Asia, he received the Distinguished Flying Cross, the Air Medal with twelve oak leaf clusters, and the Purple Heart. After his return to the U.S., he was assigned to Nellis AFB where he flew as a rightseater in the F-111A. He left the Air Force at the end of February, 1977.

In March, 1977 Don went to work for North American Aircraft Division of Rockwell International, in Los Angeles, as a Flight Manual writer on the B-1A program. He was later made Editor of the Flight Manuals for B-1A #3 and B-1A #4. Following the cancellation of the B-1A production, he went to work for Northrop Aircraft as a fire control and ECM systems maintenance manual writer on the F-5 program.

In October, 1978 he started his employment at Boeing in Wichita, Kansas as a Flight Manual/ Weapon Delivery manual writer on the B-52 OAS/CMI (Offensive Avionics System/Cruise Missile Integration) program. He is presently the editor for Boeing's B-52 Flight and Weapon Delivery manuals, B-1 OSO/DSO Flight Manuals and Weapon Delivery Manuals.

Don Logan is also the author of *Rockwell B-1B: SAC's Last Bomber*; *The 388th Tactical Fighter Wing: At Korat Royal Thai Air Force Base 1972*; *Northrop's T-38 Talon*; and *Northrop's YF-17 Cobra*. (all available from Schiffer Publishing Ltd.)

Book Design by Robert Biondi.
Front dust jacket image courtesy of Rick Llinares/Dash 2 Aviation Photography.

Copyright © 1997 by Don Logan.
Library of Congress Catalog Number: 96-70468.

All rights reserved. No part of this work may be reproduced or used in any forms or by any means – graphic, electronic or mechanical, including photocopying or information storage and retrieval systems – without written permission from the copyright holder.

Printed in China.
ISBN: 0-7643-0147-0

We are interested in hearing from authors with book ideas on related topics.

Published by Schiffer Publishing Ltd.
77 Lower Valley Road
Atglen, PA 19310
Phone: (610) 593-1777
FAX: (610) 593-2002
E-mail: Schifferbk@aol.com.
Please write for a free catalog.
This book may be purchased from the publisher.
Please include $2.95 postage.
Try your bookstore first.

Contents

CHAPTER 1: A-10 HISTORY

A-X PROGRAM AND PROTOTYPE AIRCRAFT 8
YA-9 PROTOTYPE 9
YA-10 PROTOTYPE 12
THE FLYOFF 15
PRE-PRODUCTION AIRCRAFT 16
NIGHT/ADVERSE WEATHER (N/AW) YA-10B 24
PRODUCTION A-10As 27
A-10 INITIAL OPERATIONS 33
OA-10A 35
LASTE (Low-Altitude Safety and Targeting Enhancement) 36
DESERT SHIELD/DESERT STORM 36
BOSNIAN AIR OPERATIONS DENY FLIGHT and DELIBERATE FORCE 45

CHAPTER 2: A-10 FLYING UNITS

TEST AND EVALUATION UNITS 50
Edwards AFB, California - 6510th/412th Test Wing 50
Eglin AFB, Florida 52
   3246th Test Wing 52
   4443rd Test and Evaluation Group 53
Sacramento ALC - McClellan AFB, California 54
Nellis AFB, Nevada - 57th Wing 55
   USAF Weapons School/66th Fighter Weapons Squadron 58
   422nd Test & Evaluation Squadron 60

TAC/ACC UNITS 62
Davis-Monthan AFB, Arizona - 355th Wing 62
   333rd Fighter Squadron (Lancers) 70
   354th Fighter Squadron (Bulldogs) 72
   357th Fighter Squadron (Dragons) 74
   358th Fighter Squadron (Lobos) 78
602nd Air Control Wing 80
   22nd Tactical Air Support Training Squadron 81
   23rd Tactical Air Support Squadron 82
England AFB, Louisiana - 23rd Tactical Fighter Wing 83
   74th Tactical Fighter Squadron (Flying Tigers) 86
   75th Tactical Fighter Squadron (Sharks) 88
   76th Tactical Fighter Squadron (Vanguards) 89

McChord AFB, Washington 90
   354th Fighter Squadron (Bulldogs) 90
Moody AFB, Georgia - 347th Wing 92
   70th Fighter squadron (White Knights) 92
Myrtle Beach AFB, South Carolina - 354th Fighter Wing 93
   353rd Tactical Fighter Squadron (Panthers) 96
   355th Tactical Fighter Squadron (Falcons) 97
   356th Tactical Fighter Squadron (Green Demons) 98
Pope AFB, North Carolina - 23rd Wing 100
   74th Fighter Squadron (Flying Tigers) 102
   75th Fighter Squadron (Sharks) 103
Shaw AFB, South Carolina - 507th Air Control Wing 105
   21st Tactical Air Support Squadron (Ravens) 105
363rd Fighter Wing 107
   21st Fighter Squadron (Panthers) 107
20th Fighter Wing 110
   55th Fighter Squadron (Fighting Fifty-Fifth) 110

PACIFIC AIR FORCES (PACAF) 112
Osan AB/Suwon AB, Korea - 51st Fighter Wing 112
   25th Tactical Fighter Squadron (Assam Dragons) 113
   19th Tactical Air Support Squadron 119

ALASKAN AIR COMMAND 120
Eielson AFB, Alaska - 343rd Wing 120
   18th Tactical Fighter Squadron (Blue Foxes) 121
   11th Tactical Air Support Squadron 123
354th Fighter Wing 125
   355th Fighter Squadron (Falcons) 125

U.S. AIR FORCES - EUROPE (USAFE) 126
RAF Bentwaters/RAF Woodbridge, England - 81st Tactical Fighter Wing 126
   78th Tactical Fighter Squadron (Bushmasters) 129
   91st Tactical Fighter Squadron (Blue Streaks) 130
   92nd Tactical Fighter Squadron (Skulls) 132
   509th Tactical Fighter Squadron (Pirates) 133
   510th Tactical Fighter Squadron (Buzzards) 134
   511th Tactical Fighter Squadron (Vultures) 135
RAF Alconbury, England - 10th Tactical Fighter Wing 137
   509th Tactical Fighter Squadron (Pirates) 138
   511th Tactical Fighter Squadron (Vultures) 139
Spangdhalem AB, Germany - 52nd Fighter Wing 140
   81st Fighter Squadron 140

AIR FORCE RESERVE — 144
Barksdale AFB, Louisiana - 917th Wing — 144
    46th Tactical Fighter Training Squadron — 147
    47th Tactical Fighter Squadron — 150
Grissom AFB, Indiana - 930th Operations Group — 155
    45th Fighter Squadron (Hoosier Hogs) — 155
NAS New Orleans, Louisiana - 926th Fighter Wing — 158
    706th Fighter Squadron (Cajuns) — 158
Whiteman AFB, Missouri - 442nd Fighter Wing — 161
    303rd Fighter Squadron (KC Hawgs) — 161

AIR NATIONAL GUARD — 165
Bradley ANGB, Connecticut - 103rd Fighter Wing — 165
    118th Fighter Squadron (The Flying Yankees) — 165
Gowen Field, Idaho - 124th Wing — 170
    190th Fighter Squadron — 170
Warfield ANGB, Maryland - 175th Wing — 171
    104th Fighter Squadron — 171
Barnes ANGB, Massachusetts - 104th Fighter Wing — 177
    131st Fighter Squadron (Death Vipers) — 177
W. K. Kellogg Airport, Michigan - 110th Fighter Wing — 182
    172nd Fighter Squadron — 182
Hancock Field, New York - 174th Tactical Fighter Wing — 186
    138th Tactical Fighter Squadron (The Boys From Syracuse) — 186
Willow Grove Air Force Reserve Base, Pennsylvania - 111th Fighter Wing — 189
    103rd Fighter Squadron (Black Hogs) — 189
Truax ANGB, Wisconsin - 128th Fighter Wing — 196
    176th Fighter Squadron — 196

A-10 TAIL CODES — 199

CHAPTER 3: A-10 DESCRIPTION
THE AIRCRAFT — 201
A-10 WEAPONS — 215
A-10 PAINT SCHEMES — 221
TAIL NUMBERS/CODES — 230

CHAPTER ONE

A-10 History

A-X PROGRAM AND PROTOTYPE AIRCRAFT

The idea for a modern close air support aircraft (later to be caller the AX) was first promoted in 1966 by Air Force Chief of Staff General John P. McConnell. Experience gained from USAF air attacks against heavily defended ground targets in South Vietnam and Laos during the war in Southeast Asia highlighted the need for a close air support (CAS) aircraft. This aircraft would need to combine the best characteristics of the A-1 Skyraider, and the A-7D, the Air Force version of the Navy's Corsair II. In addition, it should be cheaper to produce than either of them. The Air Force also wanted an airplane that would have short takeoff and landing (STOL) capability from rough fields.

In early 1967, Request For Proposals (RFP) went out to 21 companies for design studies. In May of 1970 RFP's were issued to 12 companies for competitive prototype development beginning the program that would become the AX (Attack-Experimental) aircraft program. The Department of Defense (DoD) stated, "Contractors are expected to explore various design concepts for the AX which would be relatively inexpensive, rugged and highly survivable." The Air Force was considering, for the first time in many years the development of the AX aircraft by means of building competitive prototypes. These prototypes would be flown against each other to determine the ultimate winner of the production contract. By August, 1970, six of the twelve contractors had submitted proposals. The companies submitting proposals were: Boeing, Cessna, Fairchild, General Dynamics, Lockheed and Northrop.

On December 18, 1970, Fairchild-Republic and the Northrop Corporation were selected by the Air Force to build prototype aircraft for participation in a competitive flyoff for the AX program. The two winners were the only companies of the six to propose turbofan engines for their designs. This was a major factor in their selection. In March of 1971, the Air Force designated the Northrop entry YA-9 and the Fairchild entry YA-10. It was also confirmed that the AX was to be developed in accordance with the "fly before buy" concept in an effort to reduce overall costs through a step-by-step progression and hardware flight demonstration.

Fairchild received a $41 million contract for two prototypes to be used in the competitive flyoff evaluation, while Northrop received $23 million in its two aircraft contract. The difference in dollars resulted from Fairchild's decision to develop an aircraft that was as close to production standard as possible. Northrop's design was strictly a conventional prototype and would therefore require changes before going into production. The target production price for each AX aircraft, including avionics, was $1.2 million with a $1.4 million ceiling (1970 dollars). The price was based on a buy of 600 aircraft. The prototypes were scheduled to make their first flights in May, 1972.

At the same time as airframe development, Air Force contracts were let for the design and production of a new anti-armor 30mm gun to be mounted in both of the AX designs. This weapon would give the AX a major offensive advantage over any other ground attack aircraft. Until the GAU-8 30mm Avenger gun could be developed, all four AX prototypes flew with M61 20mm Gatling guns. The Avenger gun was designed to fire 30mm shells made of depleted uranium at a rate of 4,000 rounds per minute.

YA-9 PROTOTYPE

YA-9 PROTOTYPE

Following rollout of the first A-9A (serial number 71-1367) at Hawthorne in March, 1972 No.1 the prototype was prepared for shipment to Edwards Air Force Base for flight test. It first flew on May 30, 1972, piloted by Northrop test pilot Lew Nelson. He described the 58 minute test flight as "routine" and "as planned." The second prototype was given the serial number 71-1368.

The YA-9 preliminary design was centered on a rugged, twin-engine, single-place aircraft with STOL capabilities and excellent maneuverability. It carried a varied payload, was capable of long loiter time over the target area, and had high survivability against enemy ground fire.

The YA-9 prototypes' primary construction was all-metal riveted aluminum alloy, semi-monocoque with stressed skin. Extensive use was made of honeycomb structure and chemically-milled skins. The YA-9 was a high-wing aircraft powered by two AVCO Lycoming YF102-LD-100 turbofan engines, developed under subcontract to Northrop. Each engine developed 7,500 pounds of thrust. The engines were mounted in nacelles on either side of the fuselage just below the wing trailing edge. The pilot sat in a protective "bathtub" of aluminum armor (titanium was the metal planned for the production version). A bubble canopy gave the pilot a 360 degree over-the-nose visibility to reduce chances of a surprise attack and provide optimum target observation.

The YA-9 also featured foam-filled fuel tanks in the wings well away from ignition sources. Redundant flight control systems afforded additional safeguard against battle damage. If one of the primary hydraulic systems became inoperable, the other would continue to function. A third manual backup system added a final measure of safety in the event both hydraulic systems failed.

Maintenance was "designed into" the aircraft. All servicing functions could be performed at ground level. The easily replaced engines were chest-high on either side of the fuselage. Engine removal and installation was timed taking less than 60 minutes.

The 58-foot span wing was equipped with ten hardpoints for external carriage of mixed ordnance. Long Fowler-type flaps extended over half the wing span on both sides of the fuselage. Large ailerons on the outboard third of the wing were split into upper and lower sections, serving both as speed brakes and ailerons, This split aileron design feature, pioneered in earlier Northrop designs, was also used on the A-10. Flap-width spoilers on the upper wing trailing edge helped to kill lift in short-field landings. The rudder and vertical stabilizer were large, affording a high degree of directional stability. Stability was also enhanced by a pitch-and-yaw-axis stability augmenter. In addition, the large, movable rudder surface was an essential element in the Northrop-designed "side force control" system. This system made use of the rudder and asymmetric application of the split-aileron speed brakes to provide sideward forces to the aircraft without need for banking. Yaw control by differential use of split ailerons was later used by Northrop to control yaw in the tail less B-2.

Ability to displace the aircraft sidewards without banking and S-turning eliminated the resultant yawing and pitching reactions that could delay or upset target tracking. Studies showed that in a 45-degree bombing run, the YA-9 could achieve up to twice the tracking accuracy with "side force control" than without it.

The A-9A's horizontal stabilizer was positioned midway on the vertical stabilizer to keep it out of the downwash from the wing and engine exhaust. (Northrop Photo)

Using double ejector racks, eighteen MK-82 500 pound bombs could be carried by the A-9A. (Northrop Photo)

Resembling a large version of the AT-37, the Northrop A-9A could carry a total of 16,000 pounds of ordnance using the five pylons under each wing. (Northrop Photo)

The production version of the A-9 was to use the GAU-8 30mm Gatling-type cannon then under development. This cannon was to be mounted in the belly, its barrel extending through a slot in the fuselage beneath the cockpit to a point just ahead of the off-center nose gear. The gun was mounted along the longitudinal centerline of the fuselage to eliminate recoil effects about the yaw axis. As a result of gun location, the nose landing gear was displaced one foot to the left of the centerline. For the flight and evaluation tests, both YA-9 prototypes were equipped with a single 20mm gun.

Following development flight tests by the company, both YA-9 prototypes were turned over to the Air Force in the fall of 1972 for flight evaluation. Over a period of two months, a joint USAF test team flew the YA-9s extensively in gunnery and bombing tests. While the YA-9A was assessed to be an excellent aircraft, it did not win the production contract.

The YA-9A supported Northrop's belief that a close air support fighter could be built for $1.4 million flyaway price in 1970 dollars. Both YA-9 prototypes were eventually transferred to NASA for its own aerodynamic test programs, and later placed in museums. The first prototype 71-1367 was displayed in Merced, California at the museum adjacent to the now closed Castle AFB. 71-1367 is now at Edwards AFB, as part of the AFFTC Museum collection. The second aircraft, 71-1368 is on display at the March AFB, California museum.

CHAPTER 1: A-10 HISTORY

YA-10 PROTOTYPE

The first YA-10 (serial number 71-1369) made its initial test flight at Edwards AFB, California, on May 10, 1972. The second prototype (71-1370) first flew on July 21. The flight-tests continued until mid-October.

With the primary anti-armor weapon being the GAU-8 30 mm cannon, the A-10, like the A-9, was designed around the GAU-8. As with the YA-9, the large size of the gun and its requirement to be mounted on the centerline of the aircraft forced an off-center location of the nose gear.

The aircraft has structural and aerodynamic features maximizing both survivability and maneuverability. The wings were mounted low on the fuselage allowing easy loading of the eleven armament pylons, capable of carrying a wide variety of weapons. The main landing gear was located in pods, mounted on the wing ahead of the main spar. The wide track improved rough field operations. The aircraft also had capability for the installation of a pylon on the right side of the fuselage below the cockpit to carry the Pave Penny AN/AA-35(V) Laser Target Identification set, then carried by the A-7D.

The TF-34 turbofan engines built by General Electric were housed on opposite sides of the aircraft in nacelles on pylons extending above the wings and away from the lower fuselage. Mounting the engines on opposite sides of the fuselage reduced the possibility that damage to one engine would effect the other, and allowed the fuselage and wings to help mask both engines from ground fire. This design, locating the inlets high above the wing line, made them less susceptible to damage from FOD (Foreign Object Damage) and other debris during takeoff. In addition, due to their position, the engines could be running while ground crews safely reloaded and refueled the aircraft.

The YA-10's engines were the same basic engine used by the Lockheed S-3A Viking. The TF-34s had a higher thrust than the Lycoming F102s used on the YA-9, and were more expensive. The General Electric Company became an Air Force co-contractor (not a Fairchild subcontractor), for the development of the improved TF-34-100 version for the A-10A.

As with the YA-9, the YA-10 cockpit was enclosed in a titanium armor "bathtub" to protect the pilot and critical components from enemy ground fire. The aircraft had triple redundancy for its flight control system, dual hydraulic lines and a backup manual control system. The fuel tanks were and self-sealing and designed not to explode when hit.

The aircraft was advertised as being able to fly back home if it lost one engine, lost part of one wing and part of the tail section. This claim was substantiated on production aircraft by battle damaged aircraft during Desert Storm. The empennage had a dual vertical tail which aided in the aircraft's stability and maneuverability as well as helping to mask from detection the infrared heat of the engine.

The programmed A-10 avionics included TACAN, radar, an Identification Friend or Foe (IFF) system and expendable countermeasures such as chaff and flares, and a Radar Homing And Warning (RHAW) system. It had a Heads up Display (HUD) that could be used for locating and tracking targets for attack. The YA-10, which did not carry equipment for night attack missions, was considered a daytime attack aircraft and, in comparison to the other attack and fighter aircraft, was much less complicated. This simple design improved its overall reliability and maintainability.

The first YA-10 was retired on April 15, 1975, after 467 flights and 590.9 flight hours. The airframe was shipped to Rome Air Development Center, Griffiss Air Force Base, New York, where it was used as a ground based tool for electronic countermeasures development.

The second YA-10 prototype was placed in flyable storage on June 13, 1975. Shortly afterward, it was transferred to the Air Force Orientation Group (AFOG) and sent around the country as part of a traveling static display. It is now on exhibit at the Air Force Museum at Wright-Patterson AFB, Ohio.

YA-10 PROTOTYPE

71-1369 was the first of the two YA-10A prototypes and was first displayed to the public at Edwards Air Force Base on May 21, 1972. (Craig Kaston Collection)

Both prototypes were originally painted gloss aircraft gray (FS 16473) and had a long flight test pitot boom mounted on top of the nose on the right side. (Craig Kaston Collection)

This view shows the 20mm M61 cannon mounted offset in the nose. The 30mm GAU-8A at this time was still under development and not available for installation in the prototypes. (Craig Kaston Collection)

CHAPTER 1: A-10 HISTORY

The YA-10's nose landing gear was offset to the right to allow room for installation of the GAU-8A cannon on the aircraft centerline.

Seen here in September 1975, 71-1369 has had a large GAU-8A fairing added to the nose and the flight test pitot boom has been removed.

71-1370 the second YA-10, photographed here in March of 1974, was painted gunship gray FS 36118 for its evaluation flyoff with the A-7D which occurred in April and May of the same year. (Mick Roth)

THE FLYOFF

THE FLYOFF

Air Force testing of the YA-9 and YA-10 began at Edwards AFB in October, 1972. Pilots from Air Force Systems Command and Tactical Air Command flew the YA-9 for 307.6 hours, and the YA-10 for 328.1 hours before the evaluations were completed in early December, 1972.

Throughout the flyoff, differences between the competitors were identified and explored in a series of difficult flying profiles. On January 18, 1973, the Office of the Secretary of Defense announced the selection of the A-10 design as winner of the A-X competition, and approved full-scale development of the A-10A.

Very little difference in weapons delivery accuracy existed between the two designs, but the A-10 design exhibited superior ground handling qualities and had easier hardpoint access under a wing with more room for ordnance. As a result of Fairchild's gamble of asking for more money for their initial prototypes, the YA-10 design was closer to production, with a simpler design and requiring less transition difficulty in bringing the aircraft into full production. It appeared likely this would keep the flyaway cost closer to the then estimated $1.4 million per aircraft.

On the first of March, 1973, Fairchild Industries was awarded a $159,279,888 cost-plus-incentive-fee contract to continue prototype aircraft testing, and to develop and build 10 preproduction aircraft. Concurrently, General Electric was awarded a $27,666,900 firm fixed price incentive contract for development of 32 TF-34 engines to power the A-10. Cost of the A-10 was expected to be $1.5 million per airplane in 1970 dollars, based on a buy of 600 aircraft, to be delivered at the rate of 20 per month, once production got underway. Costs were stated in 1970 dollars.

On June 21, 1973 the Air Force announced the completion of contract negotiations with General Electric for the GAU-8 cannon. They were awarded a $23,754,567 firm fixed price incentive contract for three preproduction models to be used for quality testing and eight preproduction models to be installed in the A-10As.

71-1370 had its left outer wing and left vertical stabilizer painted white for photographic orientation during spin tests. (Tom Brewer)

CHAPTER 1: A-10 HISTORY

PRE-PRODUCTION AIRCRAFT

Before full scale production of the A-10A could begin a political problem had to be overcome. The Texas congressional delegation, looking out for their home districts, was pushing the older A-7D aircraft as being able to meet the close air support (CAS) mission requirements. The A-7 was built by Ling Temco Vought (LTV) in the Dallas/Forth Worth, Texas area. The Texas delegation argued that the A-7D was a proven aircraft and was currently in production, and would therefore be cheaper to obtain in the numbers needed to meet the requirement than the new A-10 aircraft.

As a result of the Texas challenge, the Senate Armed Services Committee withheld 30 million dollars originally programmed for the long lead items for the first A-10 production lot, and both the House and the Senate required another flyoff be conducted, this time between the A-10 and the A-7D.

The second flyoff began on April 15, 1974. Held at McConnell AFB, Kansas, Army ranges at Fort Riley in north central Kansas, were used to make simulated attacks on ground targets. An A-7D and the second prototype YA-10 were used in this flyoff. The YA-10 prototype had not yet had a 30mm gun installed, nor were its head-up display (HUD), Maverick launch system, or countermeasures equipment installed. Four Air Force pilots with close-air combat time flew both test aircraft, and were backed by a team of TAC and AF Systems Command ground observers. The pilots came from F-100s or F-4s, with none having A-7 or A-10 experience. In one test, with both aircraft carrying eighteen 500 pound bombs on a 260 nautical mile mission, the A-10 remained on station for two hours compared to the A-7's eleven minutes. As expected, the A-10 was found to have greater lethality, a better chance of surviving, and less expensive aircraft to operate. The report was delivered to Congress in June, 1974.

It was decided that the A-10 was the better aircraft for the CAS mission, particularly in its ability to spot targets in less than ideal conditions. Deputy Secretary of Defense William Clements testified before Congress that the flyoff results were unanimous in favor of the A-10. The program was resumed with full expectations for production. Congress approved a military appropriations bill that allocated 138 million dollars for the aircraft production lot with 20 million dollars restored from the earlier cut.

After the positive outcome of the second flyoff, Fairchild was able to resume its production program for the A-10. Long lead items were ordered for the first production lot of fifty-two aircraft, following the initial order for ten preproduction aircraft. This initial preproduction order included six DT&E (Development, Test and Evaluation) aircraft, and four production aircraft to be assigned to Edwards Air Force Base for developmental testing. The four production aircraft were later canceled. The A-10 production line started with the six DT&E aircraft being built at the company's Farmingdale, Long Island plant.

Delivery of the six preproduction A-10As (listed officially on Air Force inventories as YA-10As) began in February, 1975. In addition to the six DT&E aircraft, there were two airframes built for static and fatigue testing. The second airframe was tested in a separate test lab area in the Farmingdale plant.

The preproduction aircraft incorporated minor changes developed during early flight testing of the YA-10. The wing leading edge slats were standardized. Trailing edge fairings which had been fitted to the YA-10s to smooth engine airflow at high angles of attack were also standardized. The preproduction aircraft also carried the YA-10's ventral strakes to smooth airflow at the under fuselage bomb racks.

The preproduction wing tips were extended outboard of the ailerons, increasing the total span to 57.6 feet compared to the YA-10's 55 feet. The YA-10's 40 degree flap travel was reduced to 30 degrees in preproduction aircraft, and later to 20 degrees in production aircraft, allowing shorter flap guides and rails at the trailing edges.

In February, 1974, the GAU-8 cannon was mounted in the first prototype. Firing tests of combat ammunition in took place in June. All the preproduction A-10's all carried the GAU-

PREPRODUCTION AIRCRAFT

LEFT: As part of the spin testing 71-1370 was fitted with a spin recovery parachute contained in the metallic blue canister which was built in to the tail. (Mick Roth)

BELOW: 73-1664 was the first pre-production A-10A as indicated by the large white "1" painted on the tail. The aircraft was painted overall gunship gray FS 36118. During its testing at Edwards AFB, 664 had the large flight test pitot boom added, this time painted red and yellow. (USAF)

BOTTOM: The MK-82 being carried for this test are painted white contrasting to the gunship gray of the aircraft. The aircraft is also carrying the AN/AA-35 PAVE PENNY laser tracking set. (USAF)

CHAPTER 1: A-10 HISTORY

8 30mm cannon (although #1 flew with an empty cooling jacket on several flights). As a result of tests, the gun was depressed slightly from the horizontal to flatten out firing passes. An automatic elevator pitchdown feature used during firing proved unnecessary and was eliminated. Gun gas disturbances of the engine were defrayed by a double baffled deflector on the barrels, and a flame suppressant was added to the propellant in the ammunition.

In July, 1974 the GAU-8 was certified for the A-10. The maximum ammunition load carried in the A-10 was 1350 rounds, giving the aircraft thirty seconds of continuous fire. In practice however, the gun would never be fired for more than a second or two. The size and velocity of the GAU-8's rounds was sufficient to destroy most armored targets.

On November 13, the A-10 successfully demonstrated the GAU-8 30mm cannon's effectiveness against a series of tank targets, including the Soviet T-62 main battle tank, at Nellis AFB, Nevada ranges.

A UARRSI (Universal Air Refueling Receiver Slipway Installation) in-flight refueling receptacle was mounted in front of the windshield above the gun. The first two prototypes had tested refueling formations with KC-135s and KC-97s using a dummy receptacles. Quick ground turnaround was eased by a single point refueling position in the front of the left main landing gear pod. Gravity refueling positions were retained above the wing and fuselage tanks as an option.

A boarding ladder was added to the left side, saving the need for a ladder as part of the standard ground equipment. Opposite the ladder, on the right forward fuselage, a removable pylon to mount the Pave Penny laser receiver was installed. The pitot-static system was brought up to production standards, with a pitot boom mounted at the right wing tip.

Each of the six preproduction aircraft was used for several purposes during the test phase, including color scheme experimentation. The primary use of each airframe were as follows:

#1 (73-1664): Performance and handling quality tests, flutter and air load demonstrations, and load to 100% limit. It was painted overall FS36118 Gunship Gray.

#2 (73-1665): Armament tests, including GAU-8, associated subsystem evaluations, and stores certification tests. It was painted in a mottled gray using an uneven overspray of white over a black base coat.

#3 (73-1666): Subsystem evaluations and weapon delivery accuracy, and was painted overall FS36320 Dark Ghost Gray.

#4 (73-1667): Initial Operational Test and Evaluation (IOT&E) performance and propulsion evaluations. 667 was painted with a special new Honeywell paint called "40% Reflecting MASK-10A." (MASK-10A paints had no FS595 equivalents, and colors shifted with lighting conditions.)

#5 (73-1668): IOT&E and stores certification tests. The aircraft was painted in a mottled white over black base coat pattern.

#6 (73-1669): Climatic test airframe. The aircraft was painted in a mottled white over black base coat pattern.

PREPRODUCTION AIRCRAFT

TOP: 73-1665, here at Davis-Monthan on June 4, 1975 shortly after delivery to the USAF, was painted in the "mottled gray." This paint color was achieved by painting the entire aircraft black (FS 37038) and then overspraying the aircraft with white (FS 37875). (Ben Knowles)

ABOVE: 73-1665 was used for weapons certification tests, seen here carrying a HOBOS EOB (electro-optical guided bomb) on the left inboard pylon and a 2000 pound Laser Guided Bomb on the right. (USAF)

RIGHT: This close up of the nose of 665 shows the mottled effect of the white over gray paint. (Ben Knowles)

RIGHT: Though capable of carrying laser guided bombs, A-10s are not capable of designating their own targets, and must rely on others on the ground or in the air to designate the target. (USAF)

BELOW: 73-1666, the third pre-production A-10 was used for sub-system evaluation and weapon delivery accuracy tests. (Tom Brewer)

PREPRODUCTION AIRCRAFT

73-1666 was painted in dark ghost gray (FS 36320) with full color national insignia. (Tom Brewer)

73-1667 was used for Initial Operational Test and Evaluation (IOT&E) performance and propulsion. (Don Logan)

73-1667 was painted with a special paint mix called MASK-10A. Under most light conditions it looked almost the same as FS 36424, but in varied light it could appear from a tanish gray to a pea soup green. (Tom Brewer)

CHAPTER 1: A-10 HISTORY

ABOVE: 73-1668 was painted in a similar manner to 73-1665, using white over black. The pattern was different with more black showing through. (Don Logan)

RIGHT: All the markings on 73-1668 were flat black. (Don Logan)

BELOW: 73-1668 seen here on October 30, 1976 carries the 6510th Test Wing blue tail stripe with white "X"s. (Don Logan)

73-1668 was also used for IOT&E and stores certification tests. (Don Logan)

74-1669 was also painted white over black, in a still different pattern than 665 and 668. 669 was used for the climatic tests. (Don Logan)

NIGHT/ADVERSE WEATHER (N/AW) YA-10B

The only two seat A-10 version was the Night/Adverse Weather (N/AW) aircraft. The aircraft still exists today as a museum piece at Edwards AFB.

Development of the N/AW aircraft was jointly funded by the Defense Department and Fairchild-Republic (five million and two million dollars respectively). Fairchild leased the first DT&E A-10 aircraft (73-1664) back from the Air Force and modified it, adding a second seat to be used as the N/AW evaluator. The prototype was designated as the YA-10B, better known as the N/AW A-10. During the late 1970s, the A-10s could not operate effectively at night or in the weather, and as a result of the Soviet forces in Europe devoting about forty percent of their training to night operations. As a result of the need for an A-10 version with night and all weather capabilities, the N/AW program was initiated.

The modification of 73-1664, the first preproduction aircraft, began in April of 1978 at the Farmingdale plant and took over thirteen months to complete. The N/AW version was 2,000 pounds heavier than the single seat version with the addition of a second cockpit station for the Weapons System Officer (WSO). The second seat was raised, giving the WSO clear forward visibility. This extra station included a duplicate of the forward cockpit except for the HUD. The flight control systems were duplicated with the addition of a second stick. To save weight, the bathtub armor was not extended to the rear cockpit. For added stability, the vertical tail was extended twenty inches, but testing determined that in production the extension required would have been only six to eight inches.

Added electronics included a Litton LN-39 inertial navigation system and dual Honeywell APN-194 radar altimeters. A Westinghouse WX/50 ground mapping radar/moving target indicator was installed under the left wing. Production plans were to move this unit to the left main landing gear pod. A Texas Instruments AAR-42 forward-looking infrared (FLIR) system was installed in a pod under the fuselage, but the FLIR would have been moved to the right main landing gear pod for the production version. A G.E. low-light-level TV supplemented the FLIR for poor infrared conditions. The Pave Penny was retained, and some testing of an AVQ-26 Pave Tack laser designator was accomplished.

The aircraft was delivered to Edwards AFB for Air Force flight testing. The initial flights, which began on May 4, 1979, were devoted to air worthiness checks in the area of control handling from both cockpits. The new equipment was tested in various types of terrain. After these initial flights, tactical evaluations were carried out including low altitude flying, target detection and gun attacks. The prime objective of the Air Force with the N/AW evaluator was to determine if the additional equipment could be handled by the pilot alone. This could lead into enhanced single-seat A-10s being developed by retrofitting the A-10 fleet. Fairchild felt that the N/AW function was a two-man job.

Cost estimate for conversion of an A-10 to the two seat N/AW configuration was $500,000 for the conversion to the two seat airframe, and another million dollars for the Night/Adverse Weather avionics. The Air Force decided the need did not justify the cost, and as a result no other two seat A-10s were built or converted, however some of the N/AW equipment was later added to the single seat A-10s.

NIGHT/ADVERSE WEATHER (N/AW) YA-10B

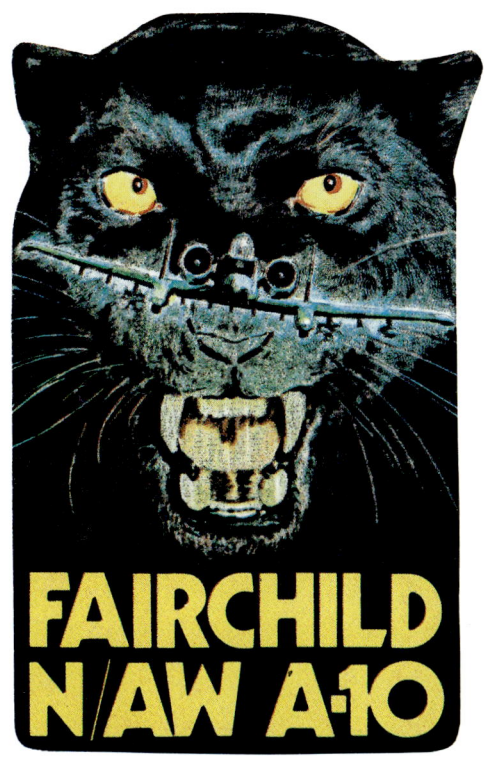

Though Fairchild used a black panther for the N/AW A-10 (left), the unit at Edwards painted an owl carrying an umbrella on the nose of 73-1664 (above). In the owls eyes were the words FLIR and LASER, with N/AWE on its chest, and carrying a seven barreled revolver representing the GAU-8. (Craig Kaston)

ABOVE: After flight test was completed, the YA-10B was retired to the Edwards AFB museum. (P.D.Snow via Craig Kaston)

RIGHT: The canopies, differing from the A-10A, were hinged on the right side. (Craig Kaston Collection)

CHAPTER 1: A-10 HISTORY

ABOVE: The YA-10B carried a long pitot boom like the early test A-10As. (USAF)

RIGHT: The YA-10B had an enlarged vertical stabilizer. (Craig Kaston)

BELOW: 73-1664 was put on display at the Edwards AFB air show held on September 20, 1981. (Mick Roth)

26

PRODUCTION A-10As

On July 31, 1974 DoD released $39 million to allow Fairchild to proceed with production of 52 A-10s, subject to the provision that contract options to procure a smaller quantity would be kept open. Three months later, the military qualification tests were competed on the TF-34-100 engines, and they were cleared for use in production A-10 aircraft.

Production continued through aircraft buys in 1975, 1976, 1977, 1978, 1979, 1980, 1981, and 1982. A total of 2 prototype, 6 preproduction, and 707 production A-10s were manufactured.

```
71-1369 - 71-1370   Prototypes (2)
73-1664 - 73-1673   Preproduction (6)
          (1670 - 1673 canceled)
75-0258 - 75-0279   Production (22)
75-0280 - 75-0309   Production (30)
76-0512 - 76-0554   Production (43)
77-0177 - 77-0276   Production (100)
78-0582 - 78-0725   Production (144)
79-0082 - 79-0243   Production (144)
80-0140 - 80-0283   Production (144)
81-0939 - 81-0998   Production (60)
82-0646 - 82-0665   Production (20)
```

The A-10's simple construction techniques kept tooling costs down. Standard conical or flat shapes were used for skin surfaces with few compound curves. This simple design kept the need for elaborate manufacturing tooling to a minimum. The aircraft had a large number of interchangeable components which could be used on the left and right side of the airframe. The vertical fins, rudders, main landing gear, wing panels, fuselage sections and pylons were interchangeable. The A-10 was the first Air Force twin jet-engined aircraft designed with neutral engines, that is the engine was assembled is a single configuration which could be installed in either the right or left nacelle.

The production A-10A was quite similar to the prototypes. A fully loaded A-10A can reach a maximum speed of 450 knots or 518 miles per hour, well below supersonic range. Typical loiter speed of the aircraft in a combat profile was around 390 to 400 miles an hour. Slower speeds were more desirable in attacking armor targets. This slower speed became a sticking point for the Air Force, which was used to high speed aircraft, and this negative image of the A-10 would haunt it until the results of Desert Storm.

The aircraft's empty operating weight is 28,000 pounds and with the full compliment of weapons and fuel this weight increased to a maximum of 47,000 pounds. With four bombs, full 30mm ammunition load and 4,000 pounds of fuel, the aircraft could take off on an unimproved runway that was 1,900 feet long. At maximum takeoff weight, the runway distance required was 4,500 feet, far below that of most modern fighter aircraft.

In August, 1974, the Air Force announced selection of the 333rd Tactical Fighter Training Squadron, Davis-Monthan AFB, Arizona, as the first unit to receive the A-10A, with deliveries to begin in April, 1976.

The first production A-10 (A-10 #7 Serial Number 75-0258) made its maiden flight at Fairchild-Republic's Farmingdale, Long Island, N.Y. plant on October 21, 1975. This aircraft and the next two were sent to Edwards AFB to join the A-10 test program.

In addition to the six DT&E aircraft, the first four production aircraft (numbers 7 through 10) were built entirely at the Farmingdale facility. After aircraft 10, the subassembly work was divided between Farmingdale and the Fairchild's Hagerstown, Maryland final assembly plant. Flight testing was accomplished at Hagerstown because Fairchild no longer owned the adjacent Republic airport in Farmingdale. The initial rate of production was one aircraft per month reaching a maximum rate of fourteen aircraft per month by 1980.

Early in 1976, the A-10 had already picked up nickname that is was to keep. The ground personnel and pilots were calling it Warthog in honor of its general ugliness, and specifically because of the wart-like round-head rivets on the aft fuselage.

In February, 1976, the DoD authorized the Air Force to increase production to 15 aircraft per month, and the fourth production aircraft was delivered directly to the 355th TFTW at Davis-Monthan, then transferred to Edwards AFB.

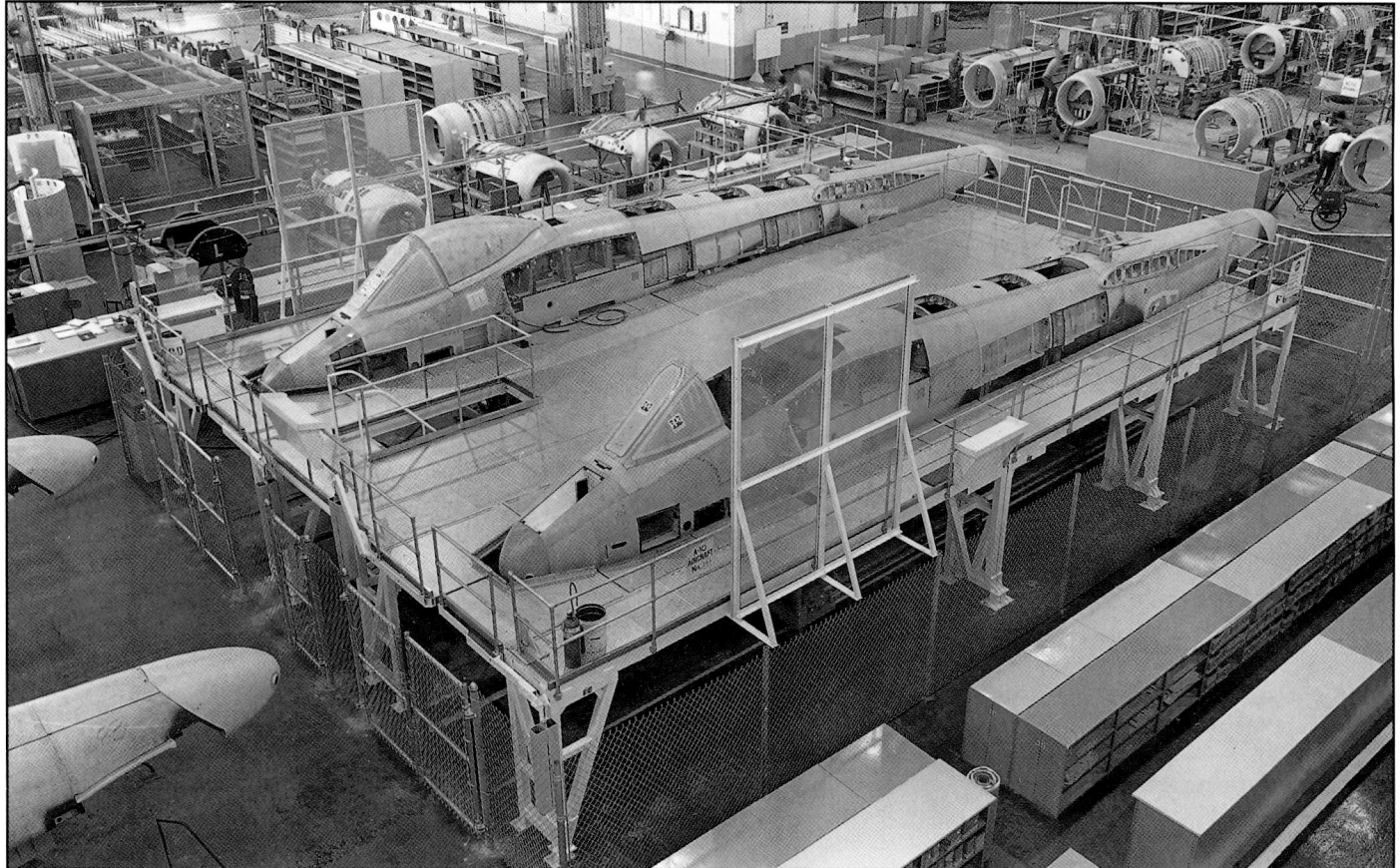

PRODUCTION A-10s

PRODUCTION A-10s

75-0258, the first production A-10A was painted an overall Light Ghost Gray (FS 36375) with flat black markings. (Don Logan)

Along with 75-0258, 75-0259 in the same light ghost gray was flown out of Edwards AFB during early 1976 for continued testing. (Don Logan)

75-0262 was painted with a 40% mask 10A upper surface and a Dark Ghost Gray (FS 36320) on the lower surfaces. (Don Logan)

CHAPTER 1: A-10 HISTORY

The first production color scheme appeared on 75-0263 seen at Davis Monthan in June of 1976. (Mick Roth)

75-0263 through 75-0279 (75-0264 seen here), wore the same paint scheme applied at the factory. (Mick Roth)

During 1976 some of the A-10s were marked with the U.S. Bicentennial emblem. (Mick Roth)

A-10 INITIAL OPERATIONS

In March, 1976 the Air Force announced that the first operational A-10 Air Combat Wing would be the 354th at Myrtle Beach AFB, South Carolina. That same month AFSC completed their testing of the A-10, turning it over officially to TAC.

In August, 1976, at Davis-Monthan AFB, the A-10 began its final operational test and evaluation hosted by the 355th TFTW. In September of 1976, the A-10 flew to England for the Farnborough Air Show, and continued on to the European Continent for a tour of key military installations. While is Europe, USAFE was able to confirm that the A-10 was fully compatible with NATO's Third Generation Aircraft Protective Shelters. It was tested in the European battle scenario, working with OV-10 FAC's, during Operation Reforger in Germany.

During November and December, 1976, additional testing of the A-10's low ceiling/poor visibility capabilities was conducted at Fort Lewis, Washington. During Operation Jack Frost, the following month, Arctic testing occurred at Eielson AFB, Alaska. Two A-10s demonstrated their sortie surge capability in February, 1977, each flying 17 missions in an eleven hour period. Each mission covered a distance of 120 nautical miles, and included delivery of four 500 pound bombs, and making two 30mm strafe passes.

In April and May, 1977, four A-10s from the 333rd TFTS participated in Red Flag 77-76/Irwin II, in the California desert at Fort Irwin. The exercise, the largest exercise the A-10 had participated in up to that time, demonstrated the A-10's operational effectiveness and ability to survive under battle field conditions against armor threats. The A-10s operated from the Army's Bicycle Dry Lake air strip, and coordinated their operations with Air Force, Navy, Marine Corps, and Army aircraft. Threats were simulated on the Nellis AFB range complex, which has the capability of simulating all known Warsaw Pact anti-aircraft threats, and by the USAF Aggressor Squadron, at that time flying T-38s and F-5s operating from Nellis AFB. The A-10s were tracked with video tape machines through the optical view finders of the simulated ZSU-23 and ZSU-27 AAA sites. In 112 missions, the simulated ground fire was able to shoot down one A-10 with 23mm fire and one with a simulated SA-6. Three simulated kills were scored by the Aggressor Squadron aircraft employing Soviet Air Force Tactics. The average turn-around time for the A-10s was 15 to 20 minutes between missions. The desert conditions on the dry lakebed were often harsh, with blowing sand forcing ground crew to wear goggles and masks while working on the aircraft. The A-10 tactics consisted of a flight of two aircraft coordinating their attacks, one A-10 standing off to provide cover, trying to destroy the anti-aircraft defenses with Maverick missiles, while the second A-10 attacked the armored units with its GAU-8 cannon. The tests were successful, with the A-10 proving its ability to survive and deliver weapons in a tough, realistic combat scenario

The first A-10 loss occurred at the Paris Air Show on June 3, 1977. The Fairchild Director of Flight Operations Howard W. (Sam) Nelson was completing the second of two loops when the aircraft developed a high sink rate. Unable to recover, the aircraft struck the ground, bounced, hit again and disintegrated, killing its pilot. The accident was a tragic highlight of a development and test program that in all other ways had been very successful.

During June and July, 1977 three A-10s from Davis-Monthan toured PACAF, demonstrating the effectiveness of the Warthog, and on July 1, 1977, the first operational squadron was activated at Myrtle Beach. The 356th TFS was combat ready a record three months later.

At about the same time, the 66th Fighter Weapons Squadron was reconstituted at Nellis AFB. The 66th's mission was to develop the A-10 Fighter Weapons Instructor Course, train A-10 pilots in advanced fighter tactics and weapons delivery, and develop and validate new tactics for the A-10. The 66th had formerly flown the F-105G Wild Weasel.

The first Joint Attack Weapon Systems (JAWS) tests were held in November, 1977, at Fort Hunter Ligget, California. These tests were designed to see how well the A-10 worked with the Army units flying the AH-1 Cobra helicopter. In the JAWS scenario, the A-10s concentrated on the conventional ground targets, such as tanks, while the Cobras attacked the anti-aircraft defense systems. The tests were conducted in a realistic environment although no live ammunition was used. With the A-10 and the Cobra working together, the kill ratios against the enemy forces went up three to four times over that of separate A-10 and AH-1 operations.

The first Operational Readiness Inspection (ORI) was conducted by the 356th TFS at the Savannah, Georgia Air National Guard base at Travis Field, in January, 1978. Twenty-four 356th aircraft flew 319 sorties in four days, at an average sortie rate of three per day per aircraft. In target runs conducted at nearby Fort Stewart, the A-10s expended over 25,000 rounds of 30mm ammunition and 420 Mk 82 500 pound training bombs. During a validation test at Shaw AFB in South Carolina from April 17 to 24, 1978, one squadron of eighteen A-10s doubled the 356th TFS rate, flying 324 sorties in three days for an average sortie rate of six per aircraft per day. One A-10 flew twenty-two consecutive sorties without a maintenance problem, with all aircraft fully mission capable at the conclusion of the exercise.

On April 3, 1978, at a ceremony marking the delivery of the 100th airframe, the official name for the A-10, "Thunderbolt II" was revealed. Two red script "Thunderbolt II" decals were applied, one on each side of aircraft 75-0553. The official nickname has been ignored and the A-10 is still referred to as the "Warthog."

In August, 1978, the 333rd TFTS began training A-10 pilots for the 81st TFW, which was due to accept its first European based A-10s in January, 1979. Under the program name Ready Thunder, the 92nd TFS Avengers began transition from the F-4D to the A-10. Also in August the 354th TFW became the first fully combat-ready A-10 wing in the Air Force. The conversion of the 354th, based at Myrtle Beach AFB, South Carolina, from the A-7D to the A-10 had taken 13 months.

CHAPTER 1: A-10 HISTORY

During the fall of 1978, a detachment of ten aircraft from Myrtle Beach participated in Red Flag 79-1 at Fort Irwin, California, another eight traveled to Hawaii for Cope Elite, and others participating in Joint Air Attack Team III at Fort Knox and Gallant Eagle at Tyndall AFB, Florida. Throughout 1978, A-10s of the 354th TFW, 355th TFW and 57th FWW had traveled to Army Posts throughout continental U.S. demonstrating the A-10's close support capabilities. By the end of the year, the new camouflage scheme of two shades of green and dark grey, called European I (nicknamed Lizard), was adopted after testing had indicated the new camouflage was the best choice under European operational conditions. In December, 1978, an A-10 from the 355th Tactical Fighter Wing at Davis-Monthan AFB, Arizona, became the first A-10 to go over the 1,000 flight hour mark.

The 81st TFW at RAF Bentwaters received USAFE's first A-10s in January, 1979. The A-10s assigned to Bentwaters would regularly deployed to Sembach, Norvenich, and Aclhorn, which were all forward operating bases in West Germany. The strength of the 81st TFW at its height, during 1980, was six squadrons totaling 108 aircraft. As a result, the A-10 became a well-known sight on European bases. Shortly after the A-10 was deployed to Europe, as a result of very high pilot workload in European terrain it was determined that additional navigational aids were required. As a result, an Inertial Navigation System (INS) was retrofitted to the entire A-10 fleet.

The first European based A-10 Squadron, the 92nd TFS, accepted its aircraft in January, 1979 at RAF Bentwaters-Woodbridge, U.K. The Squadron redeployed some of the airplanes immediately to their forward operating location (FOL) at Sembach AB, Germany, to participate in the U.S. Army Field Training Exercise CERTAIN SENTINEL. They were joined by six more A-10s flown in from the 354th TFW, at Myrtle Beach.

With the A-10 entering operational service in combat units as mentioned previously, the tactics to be employed by the A-10s were being developed by the 57th Fighter Weapons Wing at Nellis AFB. Though based at Nellis AFB, the 57th FWW did a lot of traveling, coordinating A-10 tactics with US Army Aviation units. Much of the A-10 tactics were developed in the Joint Attack Weapons System (JAWS) Tactics Development Evaluations. As the first modern aircraft designed specifically for close air support with troops in contact, the A-10 would interact with Army scout and attack helicopters. The basic tactics gave the A-10s airspace from the treetops on up, and the helicopters the space from the ground to the treetops. Both grouped would use terrain masking as a defensive tactic. The scout helicopter would act as the forward air controller (FAC) for the A-10s. The attack helicopters staying low, out of sight, while the A-10s were attacking, then as the A-10s pulled off the target drawing enemy AAA, the attack helicopters would neutralize the enemy defenses. This coordination assured maximum continuous pressure on the enemy, and simplified command and control of the forces.

Operation Coronet Filley held in March of 1979 in Suwon, South Korea, a squadron of A-10s achieved a sortie rate of five per aircraft per day with a peak of seven being reached.

In April, 1979, the Connecticut ANG's 118th Tactical Fighter Squadron received its first A-10s directly from the factory, marking the first time an Air National Guard unit acquired a fighter that had not been handed down "used" from a regular USAF unit.

Early In 1980, the Air Force announced that the Air Force Reserve would begin operating the A-10. Scheduled to convert to the A-10 at that time were the 45th TFS at Grissom AFB, Indiana (from A-37s), and the 47th TFS at Barksdale AFB, Louisiana (also from A-37s). In June, 1980, the first AFRES A-10 was delivered to Barksdale AFB, Louisiana.

In April, 1981 at RAF Bentwaters, a one day surge effort called Porker 500 was conducted by the 81st TFW. Eighty-nine A-10s flew 579 hours while flying 533 sorties in fourteen hours, a one day sortie rate of almost six per aircraft per day. At England AFB, the 76th TFS achieved a one day sortie rate of six by flying 117 sorties by twenty-four aircraft. The success of the A-10 in these exercises drew favorable comments from top level officials. Lieutenant General Kelly Burke, the Deputy Chief of Staff for USAF Research, Development, and Acquisition, in testimony at the Military Posture hearings held by the House of Representatives Armed Service Committee, during March of 1980. He said, "We get a higher sortie rate from the A-10 than any of our aircraft. It is capable of about six sorties per day and had the lowest operating cost of any of our first line fighters."

By the early 1980s the A-10 would be primarily deployed at five Air Force bases, one NATO base in England, four Air Force Reserve bases and four Air National Guard bases.

The 57th Fighter Weapons Wing was located at Nellis AFB Las Vegas, Nevada.

A-10 INITIAL OPERATIONS/OA-10A

The 355th Tactical Training Wing was at Davis Monthan AFB, Tucson, Arizona.

The 354th Tactical Fighter Wing was at Myrtle Beach AFB, Myrtle Beach, South Carolina.

The 23rd Tactical Fighter Wing was located at England AFB, Alexandria, Louisiana.

The 81st Tactical Fighter Wing was at RAF Bentwaters, Woodbridge, Great Britain.

Air Force Reserve Units included 917th Tactical Fighter Group at Barksdale AFB, Louisiana.

The 434th TFW at Grissom AFB, Indiana.

The 926th Tactical Fighter Group at NAS New Orleans.

The 442nd Tactical Fighter Group at Richards-Gebaur AFB outside Kansas City, Missouri.

National Guard units included the 174th TFW at Hancock AFB Syracuse, New York.

The 103rd Tactical Fighter Group at Bradley ANGB, Winsdor Locks, Connecticut.

The 104th Tactical Fighter Group based at Barnes ANGB, Westfield, Massachusetts.

The 175th Tactical Fighter Group at Martin ANGB, Baltimore, Maryland.

For PACAF, the Korean-based 25th TFS began receiving A-10s in November, 1981, and the Alaskan Air Command's 18th TFS followed the next month.

The following years would bring many changes and reassignments of A-10s to different continental U.S. Air Force bases, overseas bases, Air Force Reserve bases, and Air National Guard bases.

OA-10A

By the late 1980s, the Vietnam vintage OA-37Bs and OV-10As were reaching the end of their useful lives. In the eyes of the Air Force, so was the A-10, as far as front-line combat operations were concerned. Beginning in 1987, selected A-10As were redesignated as OA-10As, the first serving with the 23rd TASS. There is no physical difference between an A-10A and a fast FAC OA-10A. Because they only employ rockets for target marking and do not utilize the majority of the A-10A's arsenal, the OA-10A costs about $45-30) less per hour to operate than an A-10A. In these days of ever decreasing defense budgets, every penny counts, and the OA-10As are not counted as fighter aircraft under the CFE treaty.

The selected A-10s were redesignated as OA-10As picking up the forward air controller mission flown by OV-10A during the Vietnam war. (USAF)

The OA-10A was bigger and capable of carrying more armament than the OV-10A. (USAF)

CHAPTER 1: A-10 HISTORY

LASTE
In the late 1980s the low-altitude safety and targeting enhancement (LASTE) program was initiated to install several high-technology improvements into the basic A-10 avionics. The first addition was a radar altimeter (coupled with a voice warning system) to improve the pilot's situational awareness at low altitude. If the pilot descended beneath a preselected altitude or at too steep an angle to recover, the system would warn him in time to avoid hitting the ground,. The second major change was the installation of the same weapons delivery computer used by the F-16. Even though the Warthog lacks the radar ranging of the F-16 the computer dramatically improved bombing accuracy. In addition to displaying a continuously computed impact point (CCIP) bombing solution on the head-up display (HUD), it also provided a prediction of the bullet trajectory to the A-10 pilots for the first time. Competing with the help of these improvements for the first time, in the 1991 Gunsmoke bombing competition against other fighters, the Warthogs of the 175th Tactical Fighter Group (ANG) from Baltimore, Maryland, won the semi-annual contest. Although the victory was extremely satisfying for all A-10 pilots, it was barely recognized by Air Force officials.

LASTE added more than the two improvements from which it got its name, with the A-10 finally getting an autopilot. The autopilot would allow an OA-10A FAC to take his hands off the controls for a few moments to jot down vital notes for his briefings while directing CAS operations.

In recognition of the growing importance of night combat, LASTE also installed vastly improved cockpit lighting that made the A-10 compatible with night-vision goggles (NVGs). Finally, to improve the safety of flying formation at night, strip lighting was added which, along with some additional warts (antennas) on the tail, provides the only external evidence of the modification. Fleet modification to the LASTE standard did not begin in earnest until mid-1991 after Desert Storm. While most of the LASTE modifications were installed at the Sacramento ALC, some aircraft were modified by contractors at some of the A-10 operating bases.

DESERT SHIELD/DESERT STORM
On 2 August, 1990, Kuwait, a former British protectorate, which had been independent since 1961, was invaded by Saddam Hussein's Iraqi army. President George Bush had begun forging an international coalition of allied forces against Hussein to drive the Iraqi's out of Kuwait. The deployment of the American units occurred under the code name "Operation Desert Shield." Four A-10 squadrons were included in the first deployment and had moved to King Fahd International Airport (KFIA), Saudi Arabia, by the end of August.

The A-10s deployed as squadrons (not wings) to the Gulf region. The 354th TFW's contribution consisted of the 353rd and 355th TFSs. The organization in Saudi Arabia in charge of the deployed units was known as the 354th TFW (Deployed). The 74th and 76th TFSs of the 23rd TFW were deployed under the 23rd TFW (Deployed). The deployed wings kept the same command staff as the 354th and 23rd TFWs back at their U.S. bases. The two units were later merged into a single wing referred to as the 23/354 TFW (Deployed). The wing was jointly commanded by officers of both contributing wings.

In December, 1990, 9th AF established the 14th Air Division (Provisional) to control all deployed tactical fighter wings. Also, the wings were redesignated to more official provisional designations. The 354th TFW (Deployed) officially became 354th TFW (Provisional), though the unique command structure actually resulted in the 23/354 TFW (Provisional).

Three more A-10 squadrons arrived in the Gulf area in December. The 23rd TASS deployed joining six of their OA-10s which had deployed in October. The 511th TFS also deployed. In early January, 1991, these three squadrons joined the 23/354th. At the height of the deployment there were 155 A-10s at KFIA.

The 706th TFS, 926th TFG, AFRES, at New Orleans, was activated for Desert Shield/Desert Storm on December 29, 1990 and was the only AFRES fighter unit called and the first Reserve Fighter unit called up since the Korean War. The squadron deployed eighteen aircraft, including one loaned from the 47th TFS at Barksdale.

Before dawn on January 17, air strikes against Iraqi targets started beginning Desert Storm. Capt. Tony Mattox flying 80-0189 and LT Bryan Currier flying 79-0210, both assigned to the 74th TFS, became the first A-10 pilots to enter combat. 313 of 322 sorties were successfully flown by A-10s on the first day. Two A-10s were slightly damaged by small arms fire on the first day.

The Warthog was designed to counter Soviet Armor in Europe. This war was ideal to prove its capabilities against the Soviet-built T-55, T-62 and T-72 tanks operated by the Iraqi army, the tanks the A-10 was designed to attack in Europe.

In response to Iraqi Scud missiles launched at targets in Saudi Arabia and Israel during the early part of the war, the A-10 was used as a Scud hunter. Because the A-10 could fly closer to the ground than any other attack aircraft as well as being able to loiter for a several hours over Iraqi territory, the A-10 became the aircraft of choice to do the job.

For Scud busting, teams of A-10s and OA-10s would orbit, awaiting a signal from the overhead surveillance aircraft monitoring Scud missile launches. After a launch was detected, the A-10 pilots would trace the missile flight path back to the launch area and use their visual skills to find the launcher and destroy it. These Scud hunting missions were flown from Al Jouf, the A-10 forward operating base. During Desert Storm the A-10 recorded fifty-one confirmed Scud missile launchers destroyed.

On the afternoon of 21 January two A-10 pilots, Captain Paul Johnson and Captain Randy Goff, of the 354th, took part in a SAR (Search and Rescue) of a Navy F-14 crewmember downed in southern Iraq. Each A-10 had to be air refueled four times during the eight hour rescue mission. The A-10s successfully located the downed crewmember and provided air cover until a rescue helicopter arrived for the pickup. The A-10 continued to fly the "Sandy" rescue cover mission throughout the remainder of the war.

In addition to the A-10's ground attack role, Desert Storm was the debut of the OA-10 as a forward air controller (FAC). The FAC's job is to identify and mark targets for attack by other aircraft. The 602nd Tactical Air Control Wing, whose OA-10s were assigned the FAC missions, were part of the 353rd Tactical Training Wing. They provided the marking for over 3,000 targets during the war. During a FAC mission, OA-10 pilots would be assigned a specific grid box area which encompassed several hundred square miles. A list of potential targets within the box was provided and it was the OA-10's job to find, verify and then mark the targets with the white phosphorus rockets. Once the targets were marked, other aircraft such as A-10s, F-16s, A-6s and F-18s would be assigned in to attack the targets.

The ground war began on 24 February. On the 25th a column of Iraq tanks surrendered to a flight of 511th Warthogs which was preparing to attack. The last full day of the ground war was the 27th, with no further action on the 28th.

During Desert Storm eighteen A-10/OA-10 were hit by enemy fire: four were shot down, with one pilot killed and three pilots captured and held as POWs, all three were later repatriated; two crashed while attempting to land, one pilot was killed and one unhurt; and four damaged aircraft returned and were repaired. Eight other A-10s received minor battle damage. All eighteen aircraft damaged were hit by optically guided, ground-based weapons. No A-10 was hit while flying night missions.

The following A-10 were lost during Desert Storm:

February 2: 80-0248 Shot down the pilot CPT Dale Storr was a POW
February 15: Two combat losses 78-0722 and 79-0130 were both 353rd TFS aircraft. The pilots; CPT Steve Phyllis was killed and LT Rob Sweet was captured.
February 19: 76-0543, 23rd TASS, was shot down. The pilot, LTC Jeffery Fox was captured.
February 22: 79-0181, 76th TFS crashed on landing. The pilot, CPT Rich Biley was unhurt.
February 27: 77-0197, 23rd TASS crashed on landing. The pilot, LT Patrick Olson was killed in the crash.

The A-10/OA-10s flew a total of 8,500 sorties, averaging over two hours per mission. The Warthog's sortie total accounted for over seven percent of the 109,876 total sorties flown while accumulating over 19,000 flying hours during the war period. Flying more than one mission per day per plane the A-10 attained a mission capable rate of 96 percent, exceeding the U.S. Air Force Desert Storm average of 92 percent.

The A-10's capabilities helped shorten the war due to the high volume of Iraq war material it destroyed in just forty-two days. The following Iraqi losses to A-10s were confirmed by the Air Force (as reported by the 23rd TFW's Fact Sheet of May, 1991):

1,987	tanks
926	artillery pieces
500	Armored Personnel Carriers (APCs)
1,106	trucks
112	military structures
96	radar installations
72	bunkers
51	SCUD missile launchers
50	anti-aircraft artillery batteries
28	command posts
11	FROG missiles
9	SAM missile sites
8	fuel tanks
12	aircraft (on ground)
2	helicopters (airborne)

United States Army estimated A-10 kills much higher, crediting the A-10 with between 25 and 50 percent of Iraq's 4,000 tanks, more than 50 percent of the 4,000 artillery pieces and more than 30 percent of Iraq armored personnel carriers. The true number credited to the A-10 will never be known for sure, since there were also several hundred tanks damaged by A-10s.

DESERT STORM Units

The USAF deployed individual A-10 squadrons (not complete wings) to the Gulf region. The 354th TFW sent the 353rd and 355th TFSs, and sent an organization known as the 354th TFW (Deployed) to command them. Likewise, the 23rd TFW sent the 74th and 76th TFSs under the 23rd TFW (Deployed). These deployed units were commanded by the same men who commanded the 354th and 23rd TFWs at their home bases. The deployed A-10 assets were joined into a single wing which would be jointly commanded; this wing was designated the 23/354 TFW (Deployed).

In December, 1990, Ninth Air Force established the 14th Air Division (Provisional) to control all deployed tactical fighter wings. Also, the wings were redesignated to more official provisional designations. Thus, the 23/354th TFW (Deployed) officially became 23/354th TFW (Provisional).

Although seven squadrons were assigned to the 23/354 TFW (P), all flew with their home tail codes and markings. During the war all units added mission markings, and five squadrons added nose art.

CHAPTER 1: A-10 HISTORY

23rd TASS: The 23rd TASS, carrying the unit's Vietnam War callsign of Nail FAC marked each air control mission with a black nail painted on the left under the windscreen. Nose art was added to the left side. 76-0547 was loaned to the 706th TFS and carried mission credits painted on the right side of the nose.

74th & 76th TFSs: The Flying Tigers (74th TFS) and Vanguards (76th TFS) of the 23rd TFW used red mission symbols on the right side of the nose to keep score, (Tank, SCUD, Armored Personnel Carrier, AAA, and Truck, with a red star for each claim) The 74th flew day missions for the first two weeks, and night operations for the rest of the war.

353rd & 355th TFSs: Most of the aircraft of the Panthers (353rd) and the Falcons (355th), of the 354th TFW, carried their nose art on the left side of the nose. Their mission markings were made up of six gray target symbols (Radar, SCUD, AAA, Tank, Armored Personnel Carrier, and Truck) and were carried on the left forward fuselage with the daily mission total was added in grease pencil. After the war, the permanent tallies were painted in black. The 355th TFS flew the night missions.

511th TFS: The 511th TFSs, from the 10th TFW at RAF Alconbury, in December, 1990, traded many aircraft with the 509th, also part of the 10th TFW, before moving to KFIA. All wore 511th TFS Vultures tail markings. Mission markings were in the same format as the 353rd and 355th TFSs. After the war the 511th added a black bomb with the aircraft's total sorties in white.

The A-10A/OA-10A played a major role in both Desert Shield and Desert Storm. 77-0272 from the 706th TFS carried this nose art. (Ben Knowles Collection)

Example of the 74th and 76th TFS mission kill markings. (Don Logan Collection)

706th TFS: Although called to active duty for Desert Storm, 706th A-10s from Naval Air Station (NAS) New Orleans, kept black AFRES markings on their engine nacelles. Mission markings were red targets (Tank, Armored Personnel Carrier, AAA, SCUD, Radar, and Truck) with white hash mark credits, on the right side of the nose. Most 706th aircraft carried a crawdad on the left side of the nose. This marking was based on the 926th CAMS insignia. Each crawdad was wearing a colored ghutra and thobe headdress and carried a lightning bolt and a tank in its claws. Nose art and nicknames usually appeared on the right side. 78-0582 was borrowed from the 917th TFG, 46th TFTS at Barksdale, and carried the 46th's markings during Desert Storm.

38

DESERT SHIELD/DESERT STORM UNITS

Example of 353rd, 355th, and 511th TFS mission kill markings. (Don Logan Collection)

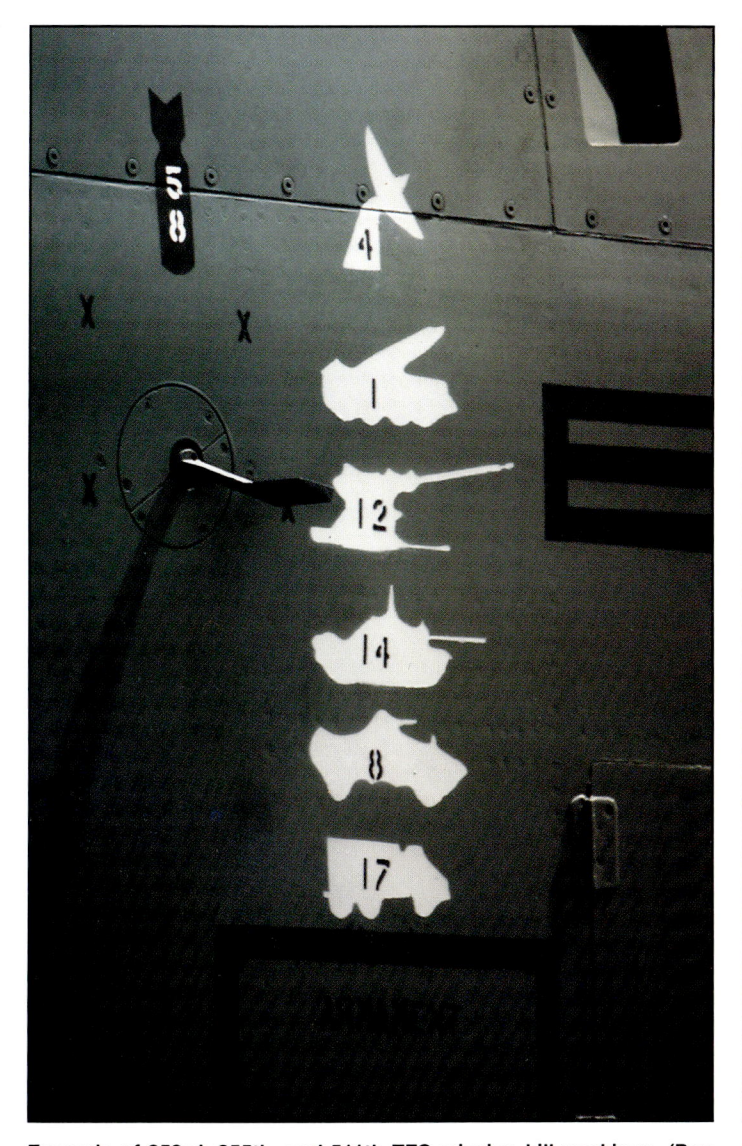

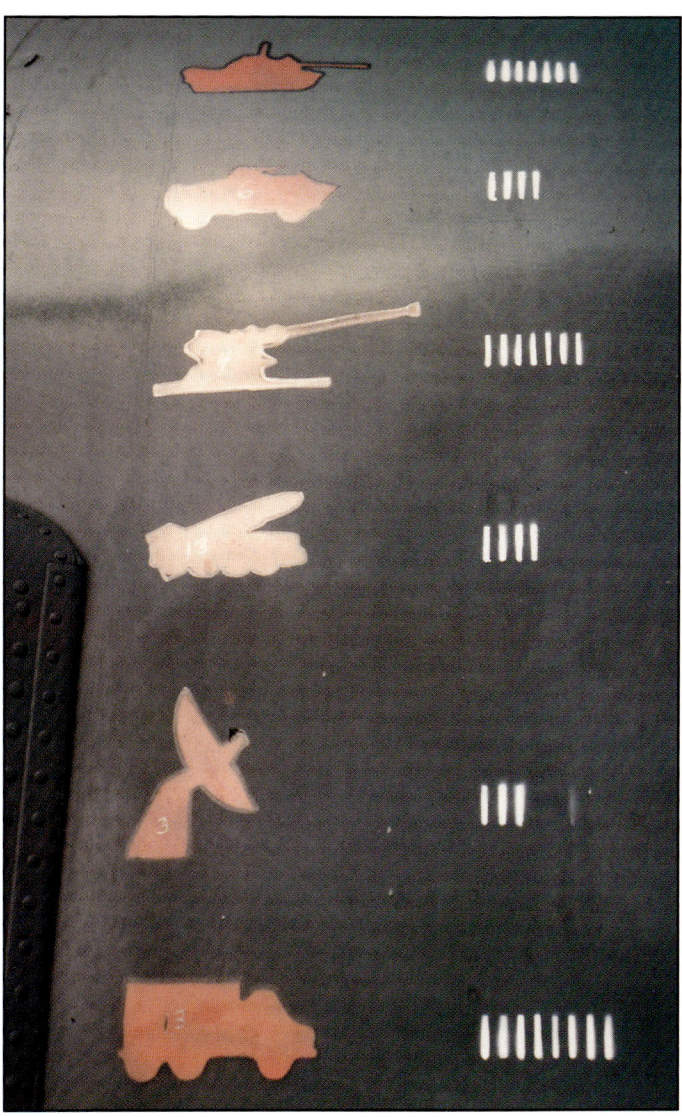

Example of 706th TFS mission kill markings. (Don Logan Collection)

CHAPTER 1: A-10 HISTORY

40

DESERT SHIELD/DESERT STORM UNITS

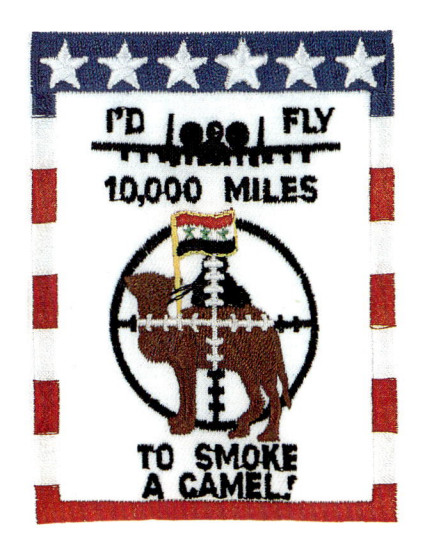

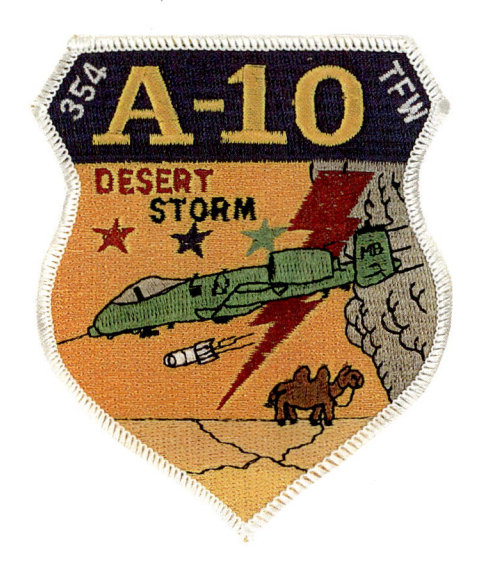

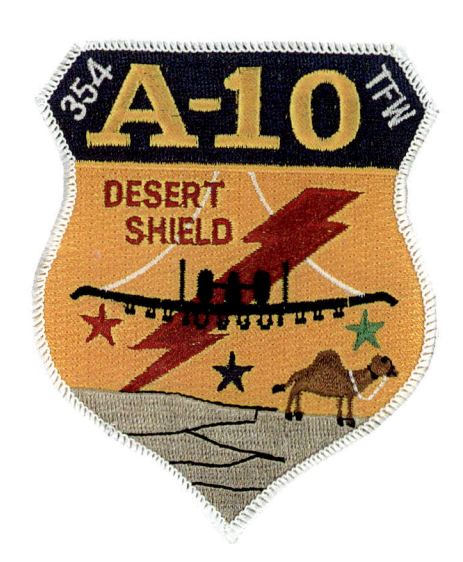

41

CHAPTER 1: A-10 HISTORY

ABOVE: 79-0137 the 74th TFS commanders aircraft deployed as a part of the 23rd TFW to Desert Storm. (Ben Knowles Collection)

RIGHT: The patch on 76-0540's tail was a result ground fire during Desert Storm. (Ben Knowles Collection)

BELOW: 79-0176 was the 76th TFS commanders aircraft during Desert Storm. (Ben Knowles Collection)

42

DESERT SHIELD/DESERT STORM UNITS

The 354th TFW from Myrtle Beach AFB deployed two squadrons 353rd and 355th TFS to Desert Storm. (Ben Knowles Collection)

78-0715, PANTHER 1 was the 353rd TFS commanders aircraft deployed to Desert Storm. (Ben Knowles Collection)

79-0158 Falcon 1 was the 355th TFS commanders aircraft during Desert Storm. (Ben Knowles Collection)

CHAPTER 1: A-10 HISTORY

78-0594, a 353rd TFS aircraft was named Panther Princess. (Ben Knowles Collection)

77-0268, Crescent City's Desert Darlyn, assigned to the Air Force Reserve's 706th TFS from New Orleans carried a hog's head in gold similar to the markings of the 917th Fighter Wing at Barksdale AFB. (Ben Knowles Collection)

76-0531, Stephanie Ann, Bayou Babe belonged to A flight of the 706th TFS AFRES. (Ben Knowles Collection)

BOSNIA OPERATIONS: DENY FLIGHT AND DELIBERATE FORCE

BOSNIA OPERATIONS
DENY FLIGHT and DELIBERATE FORCE

On July 22, 1993, NATO committed to provide close air support for the United Nations Protection Forces (UNPROFOR) in Bosnia under Operation Deny Flight. This close air support force was in addition to the NATO fighter aircraft deployed on April 12, 1993, to enforce the U.N. ban on flights of military aircraft in the air space over Bosnia-Herzegovina. The force was made up of over 100 attack aircraft from four NATO countries. This force included U.S. A/OA-10s. The 52nd Fighter Wing at Spangdahlem AB in Germany sent 12 A-10s to Aviano Air Base in northern Italy. U.S. A-10s from active duty, Air Force Reserve, and Air National Guard units cycled through Aviano AB. During early fall of 1995, the scope of Operation Deny Flight was broadened to include Operation Deliberate Force. Operation Deliberate Force was planned to employ air power to force the combatants in Bosnia-Herzegovina to comply with the U.N. peace resolutions. The A-10s played important roles in support of both Operation Deny Flight and Operation Deliberate Force.

During the spring of 1995 the 303rd Fighter Squadron, 442nd Fighter Wing from Whiteman AFB, Missouri, and the 46th Fighter Squadron, 917th Wing, Barksdale AFB, Louisiana, were operating from Aviano AB during one of their scheduled Operation Deny Flight deployments. On June 2, three weeks into the 917th's deployment, A USAF F-16C from the "Triple Nickel" (555th Fighter Squadron, 31st Fighter Wing) at Aviano AB was shot down by a Serb SAM while on a mis-

These two A-10s, 79-0154 of the 917th Wing AFRES at Barksdale AFB, Louisiana and 79-0111 of the 442nd Fighter Wing AFRES at Whiteman AFB, Missouri are seen here on the ramp at Aviano AB, Italy during Operation Deny Flight. (917th WG Public Affairs Office)

The A-10s, while at Aviano AB were kept in standard NATO hangars seen behind 79-0123 from the 442nd Fighter Wing. (917th WG Public Affairs Office)

CHAPTER 1: A-10 HISTORY

sion over Bosnia-Herzegovina. The A-10s flew search missions searching for the downed pilot, Captain Scott O'Grady. They also were put on short-notice alert to assist in rescue efforts, should it become necessary. On June 8, two 917th A-10s escorted the Marine Corps CH-53 helicopters which had rescued Capt. O'Grady. The two A-10 covered the last portion of the egress out of Bosnia, through Croatia to the Adriatic Sea. On June 13th, the aircraft of the 442nd and 917th left Aviano AB for home.

During Operation Deliberate Force, the 131st Fighter Squadron of the 104th Fighter Wing was TDY to Aviano AB. The 104th Fighter Wing, Massachusetts Air National Guard, is at stationed at Air National Guard Base, Westfield Massachusetts. The unit deployed on August 6, 1995 for a two month deployment to Italy in support of Operation Deny Flight. While

AN/ALQ-131 ECM pods seen here on the left outboard pylon on 79-0150 were carried along with chaff and flares for protection against enemy threats. (917th WG Public Affairs Office)

A-10s of the 917th Wing were marked with their distinctive Hog faces while flying Bosnian missions. (917th WG Public Affairs Office)

46

BOSNIA OPERATIONS: DENY FLIGHT AND DELIBERATE FORCE

at Aviano AB, Operation Deny Flight expanded to include Operation Deliberate Force. During Deliberate Force, the A-10s of the 131st acted as forward air controllers for U.N. ground and air forces, directing ground fire and NATO strike aircraft. In addition the A-10s were tasked for attack missions against air defense missile sites, radar sites, storage and staging areas, and command and control facilities. The A-10s employed their full range of weapons including the GAU-8 30mm cannon and the AGM-65 Maverick missile. The typical mission weapons load was 1,350 rounds of 30mm ammunition, two AGM-65 Mavericks or a selection of general purpose bombs. The self-defense load included two AIM-9M Sidewinder missiles and an AN/ALQ-131 ECM pod augmented with internally carried chaff and flares. 207 sorties were flown by the 104th in support of Operation Deliberate Force with no losses. On one mission six SAMs were launched at A-10A 78-0626, the pilot successfully evaded the missiles. The deployed aircraft returned home to Barnes Field on October 16, 1995.

On missions over Bosnia AIM-9s were carried for self defense along with AGM-65 Maverick missiles to destroy ground targets. (917th WG Public Affairs Office)

The 81st FS of the 52nd FW at Spangdalem AB, Germany also took part in the air operations over Bosnia. 81-0962 is seen, during August 1996, in this shot in front of one of the NATO hangars at Aviano Air Base. (Alec Fushi)

CHAPTER 1: A-10 HISTORY

82-0649 on the ramp at Aviano AB during August, 1996. (Alec Fushi)

81-0998 assigned to the 110th Fighter Group, Michigan Air National Guard on the ramp at Aviano during December, 1994. (Tim Doherty)

During Operation Deliberate Force, A-10s of the 131st Fighter Squadron, 104th Fighter Wing Massachusetts Air National Guard flew both ground attack missions and acted as forward air controllers for NATO forces. (Paul Hart)

BOSNIA OPERATIONS: DENY FLIGHT AND DELIBERATE FORCE

LEFT AND BELOW: As witnessed by these markings, A-10 78-0626 below, on one of its four Operation Deliberate Force missions, was locked on and launched at by SAMs six times. (Paul Hart)

78-0614 (Death From Above) of the 104th FW is marked with three bombs, indicating it flew three Operation Deliberate Force missions. (Paul Hart)

CHAPTER TWO

A-10 Flying Units

TEST AND EVALUATION UNITS

EDWARDS AFB, CALIFORNIA
6510th/412th Test Wing

The AX Joint Test Force (JTF) was formed in 1972. The JTF was made up of personnel from both the Air Force Systems Command and the using command (TAC). The JTF operated as part of the 6510th Test Wing (TW) which was part of the Air Force Flight Test Center (AFFTC) at Edwards AFB, California. The JTF conducted the flyoff between Northrop's A-9 and Fairchild's A-10 prototype aircraft. On January 18, 1973, after the A-10 was chosen as the winner of the flyoff, the AX JTF was changed to the A-10A JTF. The JTF conducted the Developmental Test an Evaluation (DT&E) program for the A-10.

In 1978 the Night/Adverse Weather (N/AW) YA-10B flight testing was conducted at Edwards under the 6512th Test Squadron, also part of the 6510th TW. 6512th Test Squadron's blue tail stripe with white X's was applied to the A-10 aircraft. In 1983 ED tail codes were added. The wing was redesignated as the 412th TW and the squadron as the 455 TESTS on October 2, 1992.

73-1669, the sixth preproduction A-10, here on the A-10 Combined Test Force (CTF) ramp at Edwards AFB during November 1976, carries the 6510th Test Wing's blue tail stripe with white X's. (Mick Roth)

TEST AND EVALUATION UNITS

ABOVE: As seen here on July 18, 1977, 73-1668 to increase its ability to be seen during test flights, had its rudders and wing tips painted orange. (Tom Brewer)

LEFT: Cartoon characters were added to the noses of the Edwards based preproduction A-10s in the spring of 1978. The nose of 73-1669 is seen here. 73-1665 (ARKANSAS WILD TURKEY) had a cartoon of a turkey holding a "7-shooter" (a seven barreled revolver representing the GAU-8 with its seven barrels). 73-1666's cartoon was "Charlie The Tuna" holding the 7-shooter, 73-1667 had a carton of a running wild goat, and 73-1668 had a bull dog cartoon. (Tom Brewer)

BELOW: 73-1669, seen on July 17, 1977, has had its wing tips and rudders painted orange. (Tom Brewer)

CHAPTER 2: A-10 FLYING UNITS

EGLIN AFB, FLORIDA
3246th Test Wing

The 3246th TESTW of the Air Force Systems Command was activated at Eglin on July 1, 1970 at Eglin AFB, under Armament Development and Test Center. The ADTC was restructured as the Armament Division on October 1, 1979. The units first A-10s arrived early in 1980. Flight operations in the wing were under the Directorate for Test Operations until the Directorate was replaced by the 3247th Test Squadron on June 25, 1982. On March 15, 1989 the Armament Division was renamed Munitions Systems Division. The 3246th flew at least four A-10s; 73-1665, 73-1666, 79-0166, and 82-0648. The last A-10 had departed Eglin AFB by the end of 1992.

The units at Eglin AFB have continued to change. The Munitions Systems Division became the Air Force Development Test Center on July 11, 1990; on July 1, 1992, AFSC inactivated and was replaced by Air Force Materiel Command; the 3246th TESTW inactivated and was replaced by the 46th Test Wing (now abbreviated TW) on October 1, 1992; and finally the 3247th TESTS was replaced by the 40th TESTS on October 1, 1992.

Though assigned to TAWC, as evidenced by the TAC insignia, 79-0166, seen here at Davis-Monthan AFB on February 24, 1981 carries the red diamond tail stripe of the Armament Development and Test Center (ADTC) located at Eglin AFB Florida. (Brian C. Rogers)

All 3246th TESTW A-10s wore European I camouflage. The tail stripe was white with red diamonds and the tail carried a full-color AFSC insignia, with black AD (standing for Armament Division) tail code. In February, 1990 when the wing began to adopt ET (standing for Eglin Test) tail code. The unit's A-10s did not carry the wing insignia on the fuselage.

82-0648 of the 3247th Test Squadron, seen here on August 31, 1985 with AD tail code, has test orange antennas on the nose and tail. (Brian C. Rogers)

The #2 preproduction A-10 (73-1665) is seen here on May 8, 1986 in 3246th Test Wing markings and AD tail code. (Ray Leader)

TEST AND EVALUATION UNITS

4443rd Test and Evaluation Group

Tactical Air Command's A-10 unit at Eglin AFB was the 4443rd TEG and was assigned to the Tactical Air Warfare Center (TAWC). 4443rd aircraft were flown by the 4485th Test Squadron. The A-10s assigned to TAWC were: 78-0715 (assigned from September 28, 1981 to June 15, 1989), 78-0599 (December 9, 1982 to January 1, 1990), and 79-0166 (June 20, 1985 to June 1, 1989). The 4443rd TEG inactivated and was replaced by the 79th TEG on December 1, 1991. This was after the departure of the unit's A-10s,

All 4443rd A-10s were painted in European I camouflage and carried a black and white checkerboard tail stripe with a full color TAC insignia and OT (standing for Operational Test) tail codes, and full-color group insignia on both sides of the fuselage. The OT tail code is now used on the test and evaluation A-10s flown out of Nellis, AFB.

The ladder door art carried on 78-0715 on January 30, 1985, is a very good airbrushed A-10 caricature. (Brian C. Rogers)

78-0715, seen here at Carswell AFB, Texas on January 30, 1985 with the black and white checked tail stripe and OT tail code of the 4485th Test Squadron, 4443rd Test and Evaluation Group located at Eglin AFB, Florida. (Brian C. Rogers)

78-0599 also wearing OT tail code, accompanied 78-0715 on its stopover at Carswell AFB, Texas on January 30, 1985. (Brian C. Rogers)

CHAPTER 2: A-10 FLYING UNITS

SACRAMENTO ALC - McCLELLAN AFB, CALIFORNIA

A single A-10 (81-0989) has been assigned to Engineering Flight Test (EFT), Sacramento Air Logistics Center at McClellan AFB. EFT was redesignated the 2874th Test Squadron on June 1, 1992, and the 337th Test Squadron on October 2, 1992. The assigned aircraft was used to test software and hardware modifications. SM-ALC had been the depot for the A-10, therefore every A-10 rotated through the SM-ALC some time in its life for major depot maintenance.

Aircraft 81-0989 wore the EFT triangle on the engine nacelle and also, after October, 1992 carried SM (standing for Sacramento) tail code.

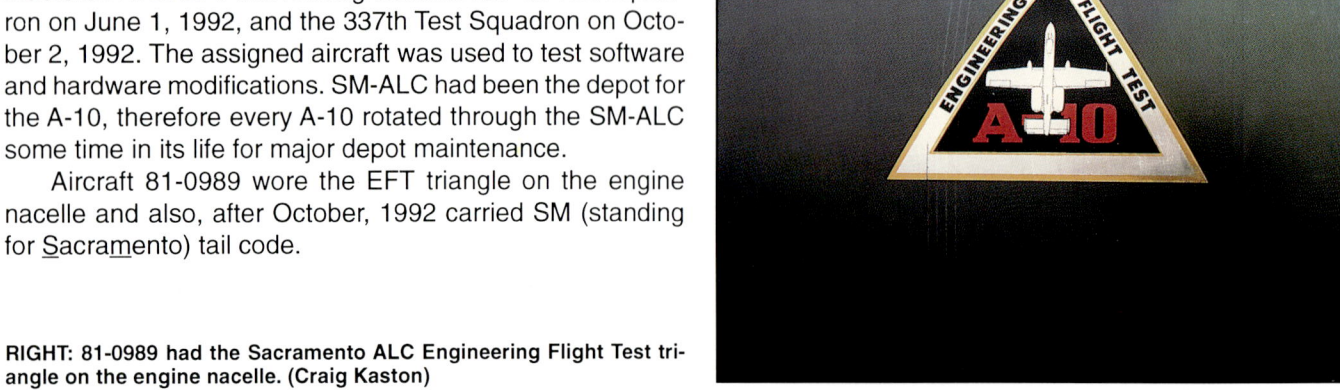

RIGHT: 81-0989 had the Sacramento ALC Engineering Flight Test triangle on the engine nacelle. (Craig Kaston)

81-0989 photographed here on July 19, 1989, was assigned to Sacramento Air Logistics Center at McClellan AFB, California. (Marty Isham via Craig Kaston)

As seen here on October 23, 1993 SM tail codes were carried on 81-0989. (Craig Kaston)

TEST AND EVALUATION UNITS

NELLIS AFB, NEVADA
57th Wing

On October 15, 1969, the 57th Fighter Weapons Wing came to Nellis and replaced the USAF Tactical Fighter Weapons Center's 4525th FWW. The 57th officially adopted the 4525th's yellow and black bull's eye insignia in 1970. The 57th has since been redesignated four times: 57th Tactical Training Wing on April 1, 1977; back to the 57th FWW on 1 October, 1980; 57th Fighter Wing on October 1, 1991; and finally 57th Wing on June 15, 1993. The parent Tactical Fighter Weapons Center became the Fighter Weapons Center in 1992, and then the Weapons and Tactics Center in 1993.

The A-10s of the 57th have carried most of the A-10 camouflages, including the JAWS schemes. All carried the yellow and black checked tail stripe and a WA tail code (standing for Weapons & Armament), and most had a full color TAC/ACC insignia. The 57th wing insignia appeared on both sides of the fuselage until 1993, when the Weapons School and the 422nd TES replaced the wing insignia with their insignia on the left fuselage side.

This A-10 assigned to the 442nd Test & Evaluation Squadron is seen on a training flight over southern Nevada. (USAF photo by Ken Hackman)

CHAPTER 2: A-10 FLYING UNITS

75-0258, seen here in JAWS tan paint scheme on March 31, 1978 was one of two in the tan scheme. (Don Logan)

75-0259, seen here in JAWS brown paint scheme on March 31, 1978. (Don Logan Collection)

75-0260, seen here in JAWS light gray and brown paint. (Don Logan Collection)

TEST AND EVALUATION UNITS

75-0262, seen here in JAWS tan paint scheme on March 31, 1978 was one of two in the tan scheme. (Don Logan)

75-0262, seen here was repainted in a JAWS paint scheme with a light green replacing tan as the basic color. (Via M. France)

75-0262, seen here at Buckley ANGB outside Denver Colorado during November of 1978. (Don Logan Collection)

CHAPTER 2: A-10 FLYING UNITS

USAF Weapons School/66th Fighter Weapons Squadron
Arriving in October, 1977, the first 57th A-10s were assigned to the 66th Fighter Weapons Squadron. The 66th FWS trained the initial cadre of weapons instructors from all A-10 units. The 66th FWS inactivated at the end of 1981, and the mission moved to the A-10 Division of the USAF Fighter Weapons School. As a result of the addition of B-52 and B-1B bombers to ACC, and the setup of a bomber weapons program, the "Fighter" was deleted from FWS becoming the USAF Weapons School in June, 1993.

RIGHT: 75-0300 in an all gray paint was photographed at Nellis AFB in 57th FWW markings on July 16, 1979. (Brian C. Rogers)

79-0168, photographed on February 25, 1984 in markings of the 422nd TES, 57th FWW, is fitted with a modified gun gas deflector, which was later removed. (Brian C. Rogers)

78-0700 photographed at Nellis on May 26, 1980 carries the 66th FWS insignia on the nose. the yellow edged blue box contains the name of the pilot "LT COL MIKE FERGUSON", the crew chief "SGT ROY PRUITT", and the assistant crew chief "A1C MIKE PADDEN." (Don Logan)

TEST AND EVALUATION UNITS

75-0269 photographed on July 16, 1979 painted in a variation of European I camouflage scheme. (Ben Knowles)

81-0985, photographed on April 10, 1989, carries Fighter Weapons School (FWS) flagship tail markings. (Marty Isham via Craig Kaston)

81-0985, repainted in gray, was still marked as the flagship of the Weapons School when photographed at Nellis AFB in August 1995. (Alec Fushi)

CHAPTER 2: A-10 FLYING UNITS

422nd Test & Evaluation Squadron

In the late 1970s, the 422nd Fighter Weapons Squadron began flying A-10s. TAC directed the 422nd to conduct operational tests and evaluations of fighter weapons systems and develop tactics for employment of those systems in combat. The JAWS camouflage schemes and the first Charcoal Lizard camouflages were developed by the 422nd. The 422nd was redesignated a Test and Evaluation Squadron and placed under the Deputy Commander for Tactics and Test on December 30, 1981. In October 1996, the 442nd was assigned to the 53rd WG at Eglin AFB.

RIGHT: 79-0168, photographed on February 25, 1984 is fitted with a modified gun gas deflector. The deflector was tried on many A-10s in the fleet, but later removed from all. (Brian C. Rogers)

80-0242, in European I carried 422nd TES commanders markings when photographed on March 22, 1992. (Norris Graser)

80-0225 taken on climbout during March 1993 with a load of MK 20 ROCKEYE cluster bombs. (Jody Louviere)

TEST AND EVALUATION UNITS

80-0226 was also assigned to the 422nd TES during 1993. (Jody Louviere)

81-0959 is also assigned to the Weapons School at Nellis AFB. (Alec Fushi)

80-0242, repainted in ghost grays, carrying 57th Wing markings. (Alec Fushi)

CHAPTER 2: A-10 FLYING UNITS

TAC/ACC UNITS

DAVIS-MONTHAN AFB, ARIZONA
355th Wing

The 355th TFW was the first operational A-10 wing. The 355th TFW had been reactivated at Davis-Monthan (DM) AFB as an A-7D wing in July, 1971 as part of the 836th Air Division (AD). In March, 1976, the wing received its first A-10. The 355th dropped its operational commitment in April, 1979, and was redesignated as a Tactical Training Wing on October 1, 1979. On October 1, 1991, the 355th's unit designations were modified to Fighter Wing and Fighter Squadrons. On May 1, 1992, the 836th AD was inactivated, and the 355th Fighter Wing became the 355th Wing the same day when three EC-130 squadrons were transferred from the 28th AD to the 355th Wing.

A-10s of the 355th have worn nearly all of the standard A-10 camouflages. Though the A-7s assigned to the wing originally had different tail codes for each squadron, all, except the very first 355th A-10s carried DM tail codes (standing for Davis-Monthan) in various sizes. The tail stripes and insignia type and location have varied with the squadron and date.

RIGHT: Initially the A-10s of the 355th TFW carried the large tail codes and tail numbers as evidenced by this photo of 75-0259's tail taken in April 1976. (Don Logan)

The first three production A-10s, (75-0258, 75-0259, and 75-0260), all assigned to the 355th TFW, were initially painted in overall light ghost gray (FS 36375) with full color insignia and black markings. (Don Logan)

62

TAC/ACC UNITS

75-0261 was painted with a 50% mask 10A on all undersurfaces, inside the engine intake, and inside the vertical stabilizer. The outside of the vertical stabilizers and all upper surfaces were light ghost gray. (Mick Roth)

The production Mask 10A paint scheme as seen in this photo on 75-0282, started with 75-0280 with all factory markings including the false canopy on the underside painted in gunship gray (FS38118). (Ben Knowles)

The A-10s started using the external tanks first designed for the F-111's. 75-0287 is seen in these two photos carrying 600 gallon, 4000 pound external tanks on the inboard wing pylons. (Ben Knowles)

63

CHAPTER 2: A-10 FLYING UNITS

ABOVE: As they line up on the Nellis runway on October 12, 1976 the difference can be seen between the early test 50% MASK 10A on 75-0261 and the standard asymmetrical scheme seen on 75-0265 in the background. (Don Logan)

RIGHT AND BELOW: 75-0264, 75-0265, 75-0268, and 75-0270 in flight over Tucson were painted in the standard asymmetrical pain scheme found on aircraft 75-0264 through 75-0279. (USAF)

64

TAC/ACC UNITS

ABOVE: 75-0292, photographed in April 1989 marked as the 836 Air Division flagship. The tail cap is made up of the three 355th TAW squadron numbers and colors. (Ben Knowles)

LEFT: 75-0308, photographed on June 28, 1991, shows the new 836th Air Division tail cap. The squadron numbers and colors had been changed to reflect the new unit numbers 357th and 358th Fighter Squadrons. (Brian C. Rogers)

BELOW: The 836th Air Division flagship, 75-0308, photographed on October 11, 1991, was painted in European I paint scheme. (Keith Snyder)

CHAPTER 2: A-10 FLYING UNITS

ABOVE: 75-0260, in Europe I paint scheme, was marked as the 355th Tactical Training Wing (TTW) Flagship when photographed in March 1990. It carries the 333rd Tactical Training Squadron emblem. (Mick Roth)

RIGHT: The 355th TTW flagship markings of 77-0224, when photographed in April 1989, include the three training squadrons, the 333rd, the 357th, and the 358th. (Ben Knowles)

BELOW: The 355th TTW flagship, 77-0224, carries full color wing markings. (Ben Knowles)

66

TAC/ACC UNITS

75-0275, photographed on October 11, 1991, is marked as the 355th Fighter Wing flagship. (Keith Snyder)

80-0235, carrying the same tail cap with 357th and 358th squadrons, was marked as the 355th Wing flagship when photographed on March 9, 1993. (Norris Graser)

The 355th Wing flagship, when photographed on May 25, 1993, carried the new 355th wing tail stripe containing the flaming sword from the wing insignia. (Brian C. Rogers)

CHAPTER 2: A-10 FLYING UNITS

80-0203, in the new two tone gray, carried the 355th Wing flagship markings when photographed in August 1995. (Alec Fushi)

80-0173, photographed at DM in August 1995, as part of the USAF A-10 Demonstration Team carries a distinctive tail cap with similar markings on the ladder door. In addition, the 355 WING is painted on the tail. The 358th Fighter Squadron insignia is painted on the left side of the fuselage just above the wing leading edge. (Alec Fushi)

78-0673, photographed at DM in August 1995, also carries markings of the USAF A-10 Demonstration Team. The distinctive tail cap and ladder door markings have not yet been applied, but 355 WING has been painted on the tail. The 357th Fighter Squadron insignia is painted on the left side of the fuselage just above the wing leading edge. (Alec Fushi)

TAC/ACC UNITS

80-0212, photographed at DM in August 1995, is marked as the 12th Air Force Flagship. The 12th Air Force, of which the 355th Wing is a member is also headquartered at Davis-Monthan AFB. The 355th Wing insignia is painted on the left side of the fuselage just above the wing leading edge. (Alec Fushi)

80-0210, in European I paint with a 357th Fighter Squadron tail stripe, marked with 355 WING on the vertical stabilizer, accelerates for takeoff at DM during March 1995. (Don Logan)

80-0212, photographed on March 09, 1993, is marked with 333 FS on the tail as the 333rd Fighter Squadron flagship. The aircraft carries a 357th Fighter Squadron tail stripe. (Norris Graser)

69

CHAPTER 2: A-10 FLYING UNITS

333rd Fighter Squadron (Lancers)

The 333rd TFS flew F-105 Thunderchiefs as part of the 355th TFW at Takhli RTAFB until the wing inactivated prior to its move to DM. The 333rd TFTS activated with A-7Ds on July 16, 1971. In March, 1976, it converted to A-10s becoming became the first operational Air Force squadron to fly A-10s. The squadron was inactivated on February 15, 1991, reactivating with the 602nd TAIRCW at DM on November 1, 1991, and returning to the 355th Wing, still at DM on May 1, 1992. During the summer of 1994 the 333rd turned its A-10s over to the 354th FS and moved to Seymour Johnson AFB, North Carolina, as the F-15E air crew training squadron.

While flying A-10s, the squadron always wore the DM wing tail code. The original squadron tail stripe was made up of red fin tips with white checkerboards. From October, 1989 until the squadron's inactivation in 1991 the A-10s wore a red band with a white sword. When the 333rd reactivated on November 1, 1991, flying OA-10s as part of the 602nd ACW, the aircraft retained the red band with a white sword tail markings while assigned to the 602nd ACW, and kept them until April, 1992, almost a year after returning to the 355th Wing. The tail stripes went back the original red with white checkerboard in March, 1993, and were retained until the aircraft were transferred to other units following the squadrons move to Seymour-Johnson AFB.

75-0265, photographed at DM on July 10, 1980, is carrying the red and white checked tail cap of the 333rd Tactical Fighter Training Squadron (TFTS). (Brian C. Rogers)

TAC/ACC UNITS

75-0293, photographed at DM on September 23, 1982 in European I, is carrying the red and white checked tail cap and the full color insignia of the 333rd Tactical Fighter Training Squadron (TFTS). (Brian C. Rogers)

75-0265, photographed at DM during May 1990, assigned to the 333rd Fighter Squadron, no longer a TFTS, carries the red stripe and white lance of the 333rd Tactical Fighter Squadron. (Ben Knowles)

80-0168, photographed at McChord AFB, Washington on March 18, 1994, carries the 333rd Fighter Squadron red and white checked tail stripe with the squadron insignia and the Air Combat Command insignia in black. (Renato E.F. Jones)

CHAPTER 2: A-10 FLYING UNITS

354th Fighter Squadron (Bulldogs)
The 354th TFS flew A-7Ds at DM between July 1, 1971 and January 1, 1973. The unit was transferred to Korat RTAFB as part of the 354th TFW from January 1, 1973 until July 5, 1973 when it returned with the 354th TFW to Myrtle Beach AFB. It remained at Myrtle Beach flying A-7Ds until April 1, 1979. The 354th remained a paper squadron without aircraft, inactivating on April 30, 1982 never having converted to A-10s. The 354th was activated as part of the 602nd ACW on November 1, 1991, and was reassigned to the 355th Wing on May 1, 1992. The 354th moved to McChord AFB, Washington, on January 5, 1993. The 354th returned to Davis-Monthan on October 1, 1994.

The squadron tail band while in the 602nd was dark blue, with BULLDOGS in white script and a cartoon bulldog on a yellow disc. Upon returning to DM, the tail band was changed to a red band with a white bulldog head and "BULLDOGS" in blue script.

80-0206, photographed at DM during August 1995, is marked with the 354th Fighter Squadron tail stripe and the squadron insignia and the ACC insignia in black. (Alec Fushi)

72

TAC/ACC UNITS

82-0653, photographed at DM during August 1995, as part of the 354th Fighter Squadron 355th Wing marked with the 354th Fighter Squadron tail stripe and the ACC insignia in black. (Alec Fushi)

81-0939, photographed at DM during August 1995, is marked with the 354th Fighter Squadron tail stripe and the squadron insignia and ACC insignia in black. (Alec Fushi)

78-0712, in European I paint with a 357th Fighter Squadron tail stripe, marked with 355 WING on the vertical stabilizer, accelerates for takeoff at DM during March 1995. (Don Logan)

76-0529, photographed on November 15, 1992 after the squadron's return to the 355th wing, carries the BULLDOG tail stripe. (Norris Graser)

CHAPTER 2: A-10 FLYING UNITS

357th Fighter Squadron (Dragons)
The 357th TFS activated with A-7Ds as part of the 355th TFW in July, 1971. The squadron's A-7s originally wore DC tail codes and were later changed to DM. On July 1, 1976, the squadron was redesignated the 357th TFTS, and in April, 1979 began transition to the A-10. On November 1, 1991, the squadron was redesignated the 357th FS, and became one of the A/OA-10 Formal training Units (FTUs). Wearing DM tail codes, the original squadron tail marking was a yellow fin tip with black lightning bolt, by 1990, the design was changed to a yellow fin band with a black dragons head.

RIGHT AND BELOW: The 357th Tactical Fighter Training Squadron (TFTS) carried a yellow stripe with as seen here on 76-0549 the squadron flagship during a stopover at Nellis AFB in August 1990. (Don Logan Collection)

With its redesignation as the 357th Fighter Squadron in October 1991 the tail stripe was changed to a yellow band with a black dragons head. 80-0176 seen here was the squadron flagship when photographed at DM in August 1995. (Alec Fushi)

74

TAC/ACC UNITS

ABOVE: These two 357th A-10s are seen here on the right wing of a KC-135 awaiting their turn on the boom. (Don Logan Collection)

LEFT: The tail of this 357th TFTS A-10 (78-0669) taken on December 23, 1979 carries a non-standard tail number. (Ben Knowles)

BELOW: This 357th TFTS A-10 (77-0201) was photographed at DM on December 27, 1983. (Brian C. Rogers)

CHAPTER 2: A-10 FLYING UNITS

Since no two seat pilot training A-10 exists, A-10 instructor pilots shadow their students from another A-10 on their first flights. In this series of photos the instructor takes his A-10 "around" as his student successfully completes a full stop landing. Of note are the partially open speed brakes on the A-10 "on the go." (Don Logan)

TAC/ACC UNITS

80-0176, the 357th Fighter Squadron flagship, accelerates for takeoff on a training mission at DM AFB during March 1995. (Don Logan)

As seen here on 80-0169, the markings of the 357th FS in addition to the tail stripe, include the squadron insignia in black and dragon's head stripe with the pilot's and ground crew names. Most have ladder door art. (Alec Fushi)

CHAPTER 2: A-10 FLYING UNITS

358th Fighter Squadron (Lobos)
The 358th TFTS activated flying A-7Ds as part of the 355th TFW on 1 June 1, 1972, and originally carried DD tail codes on its A-7s. Conversion to A-10s began in January, 1978. The unit was redesignated as the 358th FS on October 1, 1991, and became one of the A/OA-10 Formal training Units (FTUs).

The 358th's first A-10 tail marking was a bright green fin cap with a stylized white wolf head. The markings by early 1990 were later changed to a black stripe bordered with white and containing a white wolf's head.

BELOW: The 358th FS now carries a black tail stripe with an outline of a wolf's head. The other unit markings, the ACC insignia and the 355th Wing insignia are in black outline as seen here on 79-0174 in March 1995. (Don Logan)

The tail stripe for the 358th TFTS was made up of a green stripe with a stylized white wolf head as shown in this photo of 75-0308 taken December 27, 1983. (Brian C. Rogers)

78

TAC/ACC UNITS

LEFT: Most 358th FS aircraft like 80-0234 seen here photographed in August 1995 have ladder door art. (Alec Fushi) RIGHT: The 358th FS A-10s in European I had full color markings as seen here on 79-0195 photographed on March 9, 1993. (Norris Graser)

The 358th FS flagship (80-0179) with partial unit markings is seen here at DM AFB during August 1995. (Ben Knowles)

80-0179 was the 358th FS flagship when photographed at DM during August 1995. The 358th aircraft have light gray boxes outlined in black for the Pilot's and ground crew's names, with the a low visibility 358th FS insignia on the left side of the fuselage. (Alec Fushi)

79

CHAPTER 2: A-10 FLYING UNITS

602nd Air Control Wing

The 602nd formed as a Tactical Air Control Group in March, 1966. The Group was redesignated the 602nd Tactical Air Control Wing (TAIRCW) in October, 1976, flying OV-10s and moved to DM in September, 1982. The 23rd Tactical Air Support Squadron (TASS) began receiving its OA-10s on October 1, 1987, followed by the 22nd Tactical Air Support Training Squadron (TASTS) who started receiving their OA-10s on June 15, 1988. The 602nd TAIRCW became the 602nd Air Control Wing on October 1, 1991. The 602nd's originally assigned squadrons (the 22 TASTS and the 23rd TASS) were inactivated and on November 1, 1991, replaced with the 333rd TFS and the 354th TFS from the 355th TFW. The 333rd and the 354th new squadrons moved back to the 355th Wing on May 1, 1992, and the 602nd ACW inactivated the next month.

All of the 602nd OA-10s were painted in European I camouflage. They carried NF tail codes (for <u>N</u>ail <u>F</u>AC - the Vietnam War call sign of the 23rd TASS was NAIL). All insignias were subdued, with the wing insignia on the right side of the fuselage and the squadron on the left. Squadron colors were carried on the tail caps.

ABOVE: 79-0177 is seen here in 23rd Tactical Air Support Squadron (TASS) colors with its tail marked as the 602nd Tactical Air Control Wing flagship markings. The NF tail code, a legacy from the 23rd TASS during the Vietnam war, comes from the "NAIL FAC' call sign used by the OV-10 Broncos flying as forward air controllers out of Thailand. (Ben Knowles)

RIGHT: In this photograph, 77-0265 is marked as the 602nd Air Control Wing flagship. (Jody Louviere)

TAC/ACC UNITS

22nd Tactical Air Support Training Squadron

The 22nd TASTS was formed on October 14, 1988, at DM with OV-10 Broncos (having just inactivated at Wheeler AFB, Hawaii, three weeks earlier). The squadron began conversion to the OA-10s on June 15, 1988. On November 1, 1991, the squadron moved its assets to the 333rd FS and inactivated. The squadron tail cap color was yellow with three dark blue stars.

LEFT: OA-10A 77-0198, in 22 TASTS markings, is seen here on landing approach. (Jody Louviere)

77-0222, the 22nd Tactical Air Support Training Squadron (TASTS) flagship was photographed on March 22, 1991 at Luke AFB, Arizona. The 22nd TASTS had a yellow tail cap with three blue stars. (Douglas Slowiak/Vortex Photo Graphics)

The 22nd TASTS insignia on 76-0523, photographed at Hancock Field, Syracuse, New York painted in subdued colors. (Paul K. Withers)

CHAPTER 2: A-10 FLYING UNITS

23rd Tactical Air Support Squadron (Nail FACS)
The 23rd TASS formed in Thailand in April, 1966, flying forward air control (FAC) missions and using the call sign "Nail." After the Vietnam war, the squadron joined the 602nd at Bergstrom AFB, Texas flying O-2s, and moved, without personnel or equipment, to DM on July 1, 1980. After receiving OA-37Bs in 1981, the squadron, in October, 1987, began a year-long conversion to become the first OA-10 unit. After serving in Desert Storm, the 23rd TASS inactivated on November 1, 1991, transferring its assets to the 354th FS.

A red tail cap was used as the squadron color on the first OA-10A. The 23rd later switched to blue with three yellow stars, the reverse of the 22nd TASS.

BELOW: Photographed in March 1988, OA-10A 77-0223, the 23rd Tactical Air Support Squadron (TASS) flagship, carries the 23rd TASS blue tail cap with three yellow stars. (Ben Knowles)

OA-10A 77-0210, photographed on October 13, 1987, is marked as a 23rd TASS jet and carries the blue tail cap with yellow stars markings, whose colors are the reverse of its sister squadron the 22nd TASTS. (Brian C. Rogers)

OA-10A 76-0516, photographed on May 1, 1992 is carrying three MK 82 AIR 500 pound bombs under each wing. (Tom Kaminski)

82

TAC/ACC UNITS

ENGLAND AFB, LOUISIANA

23rd Tactical Fighter Wing

The 23rd TFW whose lineage goes back to the original Flying Tigers in the China-Burma-India Theater during World War II. The 23rd TFW set up operations at England AFB, Alexandria, Louisiana, with A-7Ds on July 1, 1972. The 23rd TFW's first A-10 arrived on September 23, 1980, and three years and three months later the wing accepted 82-0665, the last A-10 built. Downsizing of the Air Force targeted England AFB for closure. The 23rd TFW was inactivated on June 1, 1992, and immediately activated at Pope AFB, North Carolina, as the 23rd Wing that same afternoon.

The 23rd TFW aircraft were all painted in European I colors and carried a version of the sharkmouth made famous by the Flying Tiger P-40s of the 23rd Fighter Group, during World War II. The tail caps carried markings for each squadron, and had full-color TAC insignia applied to the tail. They also had full-color 23rd TFW insignia on both sides of the fuselage. Tail code for the 23rd TFW was EL for (standing for England AFB).

The Sharkmouth noses of the 23rd Tactical Fighter Wing, England AFB, Louisiana, present a fierce appearance on the Nellis flightline for Gunsmoke 89. (Alec Fushi)

CHAPTER 2: A-10 FLYING UNITS

The sharkmouth on the aircraft of the 23rd Tactical Fighter Wing reflects the wing's heritage as World War II's "Flying Tigers." (Brian C. Rogers)

The 23rd TFW, later to be based at Pope AFB, North Carolina, first flew A-10As from England AFB in Alexandria, Louisiana. This photo of 80-0223 was taken on October 27, 1986, while marked as the 23rd TFW flagship. (B. Greby)

TAC/ACC UNITS

This photo of 79-0196, photographed on March 24, 1991, on its return from Desert Storm, carries markings of the 23rd TFW flagship along with Desert Storm mission markings. (Kevin Foy via Ben Knowles)

79-0184, photographed on June 7, 1991, as one of the 23rd TFW A-10A Demonstration Team, carries a composite tail cap markings made up the markings of the wings three Tactical Fighter Squadrons; the 74th, 75th, and 76th TFSs. (Norris Graser)

80-0224 carries GUNSMOKE markings, including a special engine inlet covers, when photographed at Nellis AFB during October 1989. (Ben Knowles)

CHAPTER 2: A-10 FLYING UNITS

74th Tactical Fighter Squadron (Flying Tigers)
The first 23rd squadron to begin transition to A-10s was the 74th TFS. The Squadron inactivated on February 15, 1992, and was activated on June 15, 1993 as an F-16C/D squadron assigned to the 23rd Composite Wing at Pope AFB. During the summer of 1996 the 74th converted again to A-10s.

The 74th tail tops, in the early 1980s, were blue with white stars. The tail tops were later changed to blue with a white lightning bolt and a blue 74 TFS.

RIGHT: The 74th TFS initially painted their A-10 tail caps light blue with white stars. (Brian C. Rogers)

BELOW: 79-0188 photographed here on February 14, 1981, carries the markings of the 74th TFS. (Brian C. Rogers)

TAC/ACC UNITS

79-0137, photographed during June of 1991 wears the markings of the 74th TFS. (Jerry Geer)

79-0174, the 74th TFS flagship, photographed on August 25, 1991, carries the new 74th TFS tail cap of dark blue with a white lightning bolt. (Norris Graser)

82-0665, the last A-10 built, was photographed on June 16, 1984 in the markings of the 74th TFS. (Brian C. Rogers)

CHAPTER 2: A-10 FLYING UNITS

75th Tactical Fighter Squadron (Sharks)
The 75th FS received its A-10s in mid-1981. The 75th FS relocated to Pope AFB, North Carolina, on April 1, 1992, to become the single A-10 squadron of the new 23rd Composite Wing to be based at Pope.

The 75th TFS wore black and white checkerboards and a white 75 on the tail cap.

79-0209, photographed on August 8, 1987 displaying the black and white checkerboard tail cap of the 75th TFS. (Brian C. Rogers)

79-0211 was photographed in 75th TFS markings on April 25, 1981. (Brian C. Rogers)

TAC/ACC UNITS

76th Tactical Fighter Squadron (Vanguards)
In late 1981 the 76th received their A-10s. The 76th TFS was inactivated on May 29, 1992.

The 76th TFS squadron markings were red tail tops with a white 76 and seven white stars.

80-0164, photographed at DM on July 18, 1981, carries the red tail cap with white stars. (Brian C. Rogers)

The 76th TFS markings are a duplicate of the 74ths markings except the blue tail cap color is replaced with red. 80-0173 seen here was photographed on August 19, 1983. (Brian C. Rogers)

CHAPTER 2: A-10 FLYING UNITS

McCHORD AFB, WASHINGTON

354th Fighter Squadron (Bulldogs)

Activated at McChord on January 5, 1993, 354th FS was a geographically separated unit of the 355th Wing. The squadron supported Army training at Washington's Fort Lewis and the Yakima Firing Center. The 354th moved back to DM and replaced the 333rd Fighter Squadron as part of the 355th Wing.

The 354th's A-10s were originally painted in European I camouflage. The first aircraft in the new gray scheme arrived in early 1994. The squadron used TC tail code (standing for Tacoma, Washington), with tail tips of dark blue. No unit insignias were carried.

78-0685 photographed at McChord AFB Washington on December 24, 1992. While at McChord AFB the 354th Fighter Squadron A-10s carried a dark blue tail cap. (Renato E.F. Jones)

This gray A-10, 80-0151, was photographed at McChord AFB on May 1, 1994. The 354th FS was stationed at McChord, while still part of the 355th Wing based at DM, for 21 months (from January 5, 1993 until moving back to DM on October 1, 1994. (Renato E.F. Jones)

TAC/ACC UNITS

79-0201, photographed on March 9, 1993 at DM, carries TC tail codes, but rather than the Bulldog insignia of the 354th FS, this aircraft carries the Dragon insignia of the 357th FS on its left side. (Norris Graser)

80-0186 photographed taxiing at McChord AFB in July 1994. (Renato E.F. Jones)

78-0652 was photographed during a stopover at Luke AFB, Arizona on March 28, 1993. (Douglas E. Slowiak Vortex Photo Graphics)

CHAPTER 2: A-10 FLYING UNITS

MOODY AFB, GEORGIA

347th Wing
70th Fighter Squadron (White Knights)

347th TFW flying F-111As in Thailand, gave up the F-111s, moved to Moody AFB, Georgia on December 1, 1975, and picked up F-4Es. The 347th TFW replaced the 38th Flying Training Wing, an undergraduate pilot training wing stationed at Moody AFB. F-16s replaced F-4Es. The 347th TFW made up of 68 TFS, 69 TFS, and 70 TFS all flying F-16C/D changed to the 347th FW in October, 1991. In July, 1994 the 347th Fighter Wing changed to 347th Wing with the addition of the 52 Airlift Squadron. The 70th FS ceased operations in July, 1993, while still flying F-16C/D. During 1995 the 70th FS was reorganized and assigned A-10s.

The aircraft of the 347th Wing carry the MY tail code (standing for <u>Mo</u>od<u>y</u>) with blue tail caps, a yellow lightning bolt, and White Knights in white.

80-0181, photographed on August 12, 1995, while on a stopover at Shaw AFB, South Carolina, carries markings as the 70th FS flagship. (Norm Taylor)

80-0217, photographed on August 12, 1995, at Shaw AFB, South Carolina, carries standard markings of the 70th FS. (Norm Taylor)

TAC/ACC UNITS

MYRTLE BEACH AFB, SOUTH CAROLINA

354th Fighter Wing

The 354th TFW, in June, 1970, became the first operational wing to transition to A-7Ds. The 354th TFW began conversion to A-10s in early 1977. The entire wing was declared operational in October, 1978 becoming the first operational USAF A-10 wing. Soon after the U.S. began deploying units committed to the liberation of Kuwait the 353rd and 355th TFSs took their A-10s to Desert Storm The 354th was redesignated a Fighter Wing on October 1, 1991, and its three flying squadrons became Fighter Squadrons a month later. As part of post-Cold-War force reduction, Myrtle Beach was scheduled to be closed and the 354th FW was scheduled to be inactivated. The 355th FS was inactivated in March, 1992, the 356th FS three months later, and the 353rd FS in December, 1992. The 354th FW inactivated at the end of March, 1993, and activated at Eielson AFB, Alaska that August.

The A-10s originally assigned to the 354th TFW were painted the "False Canopy" MASK-10A scheme. The black MB tail code (standing for Myrtle Beach) The black-outline TAC insignias, and black-outline 354th insignias were the only unit markings originally on the aircraft. In early 1980, with most aircraft now in European I paint, full-color squadron insignias were applied on the left side of the fuselage, and tail stripes were added.

LEFT: The tail of 78-0655 shows off the 354 TFW flagship markings. (Ben Knowles)

BELOW: 78-0675, photographed in 1981, has its vertical stabilizer and rudder painted with a diagonal command stripe (indicating it was assigned to the Wing Commander), made up of the three squadron colors (red, blue, and green), with the tail cap of the 356th Tactical Fighter Squadron. (Don Logan Collection)

CHAPTER 2: A-10 FLYING UNITS

78-0675, photographed on March 10, 1982, with its vertical stabilizer and rudder still painted with the diagonal command stripe, carries the new tail cap of the 356th TFS. (Charles Mayer)

77-0202, photographed on September 6, 1978 at DM, wears the standard production Mask 10A paint scheme. The external tanks are still painted in the dark gray paint reflecting their earlier use on SAC FB-111As. (Brian C. Rogers)

76-0520, photographed on November 29, 1978 at DM shows how quickly the production paint scheme weathered. (Brian C. Rogers)

TAC/ACC UNITS

75-0302 photographed at DM on March 17, 1979 after a recent desert thunderstorm, has Boar tusks on the nose, starting a tradition of hogs heads on A-10 noses. (Brian C. Rogers)

78-0655, photographed in October 1991 wears the flagship markings of the 354th TFW. (Ben Knowles)

CHAPTER 2: A-10 FLYING UNITS

353rd Tactical Fighter Squadron (Panthers)
The 353rd TFS received its A-10s in August, 1978, The Squadron was inactivated on December 15, 1992.

The 353rd's original tail stripe was red and carried a black silhouette of a panther. After 1983 tail cap marking was simplified to just a red fin cap.

77-0680, photographed on October 11, 1991, has had the 353rd TFS black panther removed from the tail, leaving the squadron markings a simple red tail cap with the full color squadron insignia on the left side of the fuselage. (Norris Graser)

78-0593 photographed on June 18, 1983 is marked with the 353rd TFS original tail markings of a pouncing black panther on a red tail stripe. (Brian C. Rogers)

78-0715, the 353rd AMU flagship photographed in April 1991, has nose art of a Black Panthers head. (Ben Knowles Collection)

96

TAC/ACC UNITS

355th Tactical Fighter Squadron (Falcons)
The 355th TFS was the USAF's second operational A-10 squadron, becoming operational in February, 1978, The squadron was inactivated on March 31, 1992 with the closing of Myrtle Beach AFB. The 355th Fighter Squadron was reactivated as part of the 354th Wing at Eielson AFB, replacing the 11th TASS on August 20, 1993.

Original 355th A-10 markings were made up of a white tail band spangled with between six and eleven blue stars. As with the 353rd TFS, after 1983, the markings were simplified to just a blue fin cap.

76-0539 photographed on October 3, 1980 is marked with the 355th TFS original markings of seven blue stars on a white tail stripe. (Brian C. Rogers)

79-0160 photographed on April, 1991 after its return from Desert Storm with the blue engine covers and blue tail stripe of the 355th TFS. (David F. Brown)

79-0158, 355th AMU flagship, was photographed with the blue engine covers and blue tail stripe of the 355th TFS. (Ben Knowles collection)

CHAPTER 2: A-10 FLYING UNITS

356th Tactical Fighter Squadron (Green Demons)
The 356th TFS became the USAF's first operational A-10 squadron in October, 1977. The squadron was inactivated on June 30, 1992.

The original 356th A-10 tail marking was a made up of a green stripe with white borders. The markings were later changed, with the stripe being divided into thirds. The forward and aft third was made up of a green and white checker board. The center third was a white field with four green arrows arranged in standard four ship formation. In 1982 the tail markings changed back to the white bordered green band but added four white arrows, this time in trail formation. In 1984 the tail markings changed to a simple green fin cap.

RIGHT: The tail of 77-0202 was photographed on November 17, 1980 with the green and white 356th TFS tail markings. The green arrows on the stripe came from the squadron insignia and represent a four ship aircraft formation. (Brian C. Rogers)

BELOW: 77-0219 photographed on February 15, 1981 carries the full color 356th squadron Green Demons insignia and green and white tail stripe. (Brian C. Rogers)

TAC/ACC UNITS

As seen on 76-0547 photographed on January 21, 1983 at DM AFB, the tail stripe of the 356th TFS has changed, now made up of a white edged green stripe with four white arrows. A full color 354th Tactical Fighter Wing insignia is on the right side of the fuselage. (Brian C. Rogers)

79-0102 photographed on March 26, 1983 with the white edged green stripe with four white arrows. A full color 356th Tactical Fighter Squadron insignia is on the left side of the fuselage. (Brian C. Rogers)

79-0133 was photographed on April 21, 1985. The white edged green stripe was replaced with a simple green tail cap. A full color 356th Tactical Fighter Squadron insignia is on the right side of the fuselage. (Brian C. Rogers)

CHAPTER 2: A-10 FLYING UNITS

POPE AFB, NORTH CAROLINA

23rd Wing

Pope AFB, located near Fayetteville, North Carolina, adjoins Fort Bragg, home of the U.S. Army's 82nd Airborne Division. The 23rd Wing trains with and provides intratheater airlift and close air support for the 82nd Airborne. In January, 1992, the first A-10 aircraft, to be used for maintenance familiarization training arrived at Pope. On April 1, the 75th FS moved from England AFB in preparation for the arrival of the 23rd FW which was still at England AFB. On June 1, the 23rd Wing activated at Pope as the new Air Force air-land composite wing. The 23rd Wing also took over the C-130Es of the 317th TAW which inactivated on August 20, 1993.

The 2nd Airlift Squadron was activated on June 1, 1992, absorbing the personnel and equipment of the 39th Tactical Airlift Squadron which was inactivated on the same day. The 74th FS, previously an A-10 squadron at England AFB, was activated with F-16C/Ds as part of the 23rd Wing on June 15, 1993, and the 41st AS with C-130Es transferred to the wing on July 16, 1993. During the summer of 1996, the 74th FS gave up its F-16s and once again received A-10s.

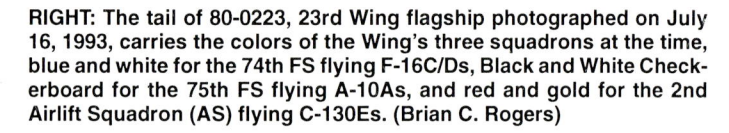

RIGHT: The tail of 80-0223, 23rd Wing flagship photographed on July 16, 1993, carries the colors of the Wing's three squadrons at the time, blue and white for the 74th FS flying F-16C/Ds, Black and White Checkerboard for the 75th FS flying A-10As, and red and gold for the 2nd Airlift Squadron (AS) flying C-130Es. (Brian C. Rogers)

BELOW: TIGER ONE, 80-0223, the 23rd Wing flagship photographed on July 16, 1993 at Langley AFB carries the 75th FS insignia on the left side of the fuselage, and, like all of the 75th FS A-10s, the 23rd Wing's sharkmouth. (Brian C. Rogers)

TAC/ACC UNITS

ABOVE: The tail of 80-0223 23rd Wing flagship taken during June 1995 with the addition of a green bar for the 41st AS, a second C-130E squadron, now carries four squadron colors on its tail cap. Still marked with TIGER ONE on the ladder door, now carries the name TOWN OF HOPE MILLS on the fuselage side in front of the wing. (Alec Fushi)

LEFT: The tail 79-0223, marked as the 23rd OG (Operations Group)flagship was August 19, 1993 is painted with two colors, black and white of the 75th FS and red of the 2nd AS. (Brian C. Rogers)

BELOW: 79-0223, in European I paint, is marked as the 23rd OG Boss when photographed at Pope AFB on August 19, 1993. (Brian C. Rogers)

101

CHAPTER 2: A-10 FLYING UNITS

74th Fighter Squadron (Flying Tigers)
During the summer of 1996, the 74th FS converted to the A-10, receiving some of their A-10s from the 55th FS at Shaw. Like the other aircraft of the new 23rd Wing, the A-10s carry FT tail codes, derived from Flying Tigers. They also have a sharkmouth painted on the nose. The 74th FS A-10's markings are made up of a blue tail cap with a white lightning bolt in the blue tail cap. 74th, in blue, is painted in the lightning bolt.

RIGHT: 79-0179, the new 74th FS Commander's aircraft, photographed prior to leaving Shaw AFB, is in partial 23rd Wing markings. The 74th FS tail cap and 23rd Wing sharkmouth were added after the aircraft's arrival at Pope AFB. (Norm Taylor)

Photographed in November of 1996, the new 23rd OG Commander's aircraft, 81-0964, the Mi-8 helicopter killer from Desert Storm, had been the 55th FS Commander's aircraft at Shaw AFB prior to being transferred to the 74th FS at Pope AFB. (Norm Taylor)

81-0947, photographed at Pope AFB in November, 1996 carries the 23rd Wing FT tail code and full markings of the 74th FS Flying Tigers including the sharkmouth and the blue tail cap with the white lightning bolt. (Norm Taylor)

TAC/ACC UNITS

75th Fighter Squadron (Sharks)

The 75th FS A-10s, like all the aircraft of the new 23rd Wing carry FT tail codes. The 75th FS A-10's markings are made up of a sharkmouth on the nose, a black and white checkerboard tail cap with 75th in white, and a full color 75th FS insignia on the left side of the fuselage. A-10s in the new gray camouflage began to arrive at Pope during 1993.

RIGHT: The tail of 80-0175 is marked as the 75th FS flagship with tail markings in black letters when photographed on August 1, 1992. (Brian C. Rogers)

RIGHT: 80-0175, in European I, is marked as 75th FS flagship with tail markings in black letters when photographed on August 1, 1992 with the 23rd Wing insignia on the left side of the fuselage. (Brian C. Rogers)

BELOW: 80-0175, in European I, marked as 75th FS flagship in white edged black letters when photographed on August 19, 1993, with the 75th FS insignia on the left side of the fuselage. (Brian C. Rogers)

CHAPTER 2: A-10 FLYING UNITS

80-0175, in the new gray paint, marked as 75th FS flagship in white edged black letters, when photographed in June 1995 with the 75th FS insignia on the left side of the fuselage. (Alec Fushi)

78-0655, the "DANGEROUS TOY" of the 75th FS is seen in European I paint when photographed at Pope AFB on August 19, 1993. (Brian C. Rogers)

78-0674. painted in the new gray colors carries the black and white checked tail of the 75th FS Sharks when photographed on August 19, 1993 at Pope AFB. (Brian C. Rogers)

TAC/ACC UNITS

SHAW AFB, SOUTH CAROLINA

Three different wings have operated A-10s at Shaw AFB, South Carolina. The 507th TAIRACW/ACW operated OA-10As from early 1991 until the A-10s transferred to the 363rd FW on April 1, 1992. The 363rd Wing operated OA-10s from April 1, 1992, until inactivated on December 13, 1993. The 20th Fighter wing moved from RAF Upper Heyford to Shaw on January 1, 1994, replacing the 363rd FW. The A-10s left in summer 1996, with the 55th FS converting to F-16C/Ds.

507th Air Control Wing
21st Tactical Air Support Squadron (Ravens)

The 507th Tactical Air Control Wing (TAIRACW) was made up of two OV-10 Bronco squadrons - the 20th Tactical Air Support Squadron (TASS), inactivated on December 31, 1991, and the 21st TASS which converted to OA-10s in October, 1991. The 507th became an ACW on October 1, 1991. The 21st TASS inactivated on November 1, 1991, and was replaced on the same day by the 21st FS from George AFB, California. The 21st FS transferred to the 363rd FW on April 1, 1992, and the 507th ACW inactivated on June 15, 1992.

All 507th A-10s were painted in European I camouflage. The OA-10s carrier SF tail codes, standing for Shaw FAC. The 21st TASS's tail stripe was blue with white borders, two white lightning bolts, and a white script word - Raven.

81-0964 "STEAL YOUR FACE" is marked as the 507th Air Control Wing (ACW) flagship, with the unit call sign RAVEN painted on the 21st FS (formerly the 21st Tactical Air Support Squadron) blue tail stripe. (Norm Taylor)

105

CHAPTER 2: A-10 FLYING UNITS

RIGHT: 81-0964 nose art "STEAL YOUR FACE" is art from a Grateful Dead record album. (Norm Taylor)

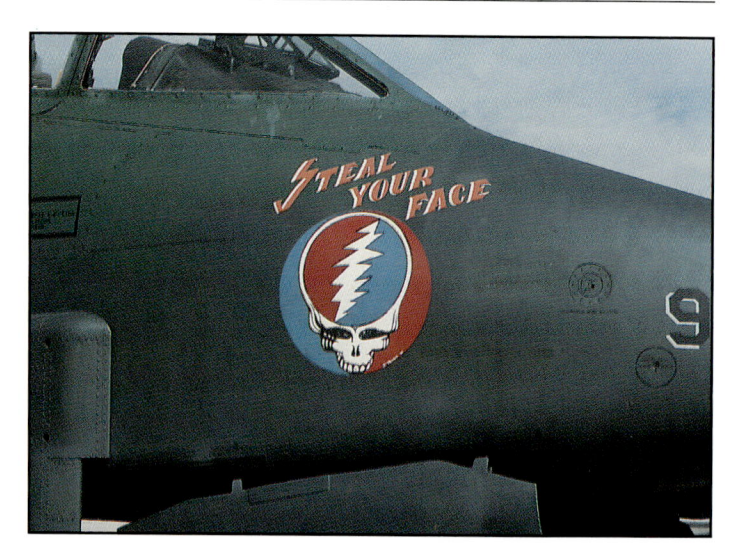

ABOVE AND RIGHT: 81-0947 "DESERT BELLE" was assigned to the 21st FS of the 507th Air Control Wing, Shaw AFB, North Carolina, when photographed on December 15, 1991. "DESERT BELLE" was the nose art it carried when assigned to the 511th TFS during Desert Storm. (Norm Taylor)

TAC/ACC UNITS

363rd Fighter Wing
21st Fighter Squadron (Panthers)

The 363rd TFW at Shaw AFB began F-16 transition in October, 1981. The wing was redesignated as a Fighter Wing, (Tactical dropped from the designation) on October 1, 1991. The 21st FS, transferring from the 507th ACW, became the wings only OA-10 squadron on April 1, 1992. The 363rd FW inactivated on December 31, 1993, and replaced by the 20th FW returning to Shaw AFB from RAF Upper Heyford.

The 21st FS carried the SW (standing for Shaw) tail codes of 363rd FW. The tail cap markings were made up of a black cap with a single red lightning bolt. The aircraft were originally painted in European I, and some had been repainted to the new grays before changing to the 20th FW, 55th FS.

BELOW: 81-0964, the 21st FS flagship in European I, was photographed in April 1993. As evidenced by the Iraqi flag below the cockpit, this aircraft was credited with a Mi-8 helicopter air to air gun kill on 15 February 1991. Capt. Todd Sheehy was credited with the kill, the A-10s second kill. (David F. Brown)

107

CHAPTER 2: A-10 FLYING UNITS

ABOVE: 81-0964, the 21st Fighter Squadron flagship photographed October 18, 1993 at Nellis AFB returning from a GUNSMOKE 93 mission. The full color 363rd Fighter Wing insignia is visible on the right side of the fuselage. (David F. Brown)

RIGHT: The tail of 80-0140 wears the 21st FS black stripe with a red lightning bolt. This aircraft has white edged tail letters and numbers. it was photographed on May 1, 1992. (Brian C. Rogers)

BELOW: 80-0140, in European I was photographed on May 1, 1992 carrying a black and red travel pod with 21st FS Panther markings. (Brian C. Rogers)

TAC/ACC UNITS

79-0170, photographed in April 1993, taxis loaded with AIM-9 Sidewinders and AGM-65 Maverick missiles. (David F. Brown)

80-0206 in 21st FS markings loaded with an ACMI pod and SUU-20 practice bomb dispenser departs on a training mission from Nellis AFB on October 18, 1993. (David F. Brown)

80-0157 photographed at Nellis AFB on October 18, 1993 during GUNSMOKE 93 carries 21st FS markings and a black outline 363rd FW insignia. (Brian C. Rogers)

CHAPTER 2: A-10 FLYING UNITS

20th Fighter Wing
55th Fighter Squadron (Fighting Fifty-Fifth)
The 20th FW moved from RAF Upper Heyford to Shaw AFB on December 31, 1993, giving up its F-111Es and EF-111As. The 20th FW absorbing the 363rd FW's assets. All Shaw squadrons received new unit designations, with the 21st FS and their OA-10s becoming the 55th (Fighting Fifty-Fifth) FS on January 1, 1994. The 55th FS transitioned to F-16C/Ds during the summer of 1996, sending most of their A-10s to the 74th FS at Pope AFB and the 706th FS, AFRES, at NAS New Orleans.

The 55th FS kept the tail cap design of the 21st FS, changing the colors. The tail cap changed from black to blue, and the lightning bolt changed from red to yellow. Some of the aircraft were originally painted in European I, though all were repainted to the new Ghost Grays camouflage.

Helicopter killer 81-0964, the 55th FS flagship Shaw AFB February 25, 1994 full color 20th FW insignia. (David F. Brown)

BELOW: 82-0655, photographed still in 55th FS flagship markings on August 15, 1996. had recently arrived at NAS New Orleans as one of the first A-10s to re-equip the 706th FS. (Nate Leong)

The tail 81-0964, when photographed on January 3, 1994, wears the 20th Fighter Wing, 55th Fighter Squadron flagship markings. (Norm Taylor)

TAC/ACC UNITS

79-0179 of the 55th FS was photographed on February 25, 1994. The aircraft has a two gray 20th FW insignia on the left side of the aircraft. (David F. Brown)

When photographed on May 17, 1995, 80-0144 was marked with the 55th FS Blue tail stripe and yellow lightning bolt. (Don Logan)

80-0144 was photographed at Barksdale AFB after completing the Night Vision Goggles modification. The aircraft carries an outline 20th FW insignia. (Don Logan)

80-0140, repainted in 55th FS markings was carrying an ALQ-184(v)-1 long ECM pod when photographed on February 25, 1994. (David F. Brown)

CHAPTER 2: A-10 FLYING UNITS

PACIFIC AIR FORCES

OSAN AB/SUWON AB, KOREA
51st Fighter Wing

The 51st Composite Wing (Tactical) was based at Osan. The 51st became a TFW on July 1, 1982. When Seventh Air Force activated on September 8, 1986, it assumed control of the 51st and all other Korean-based PACAF assets from 5th Air Force. The 51st TFW was redesignated as the 51st Wing on February 7, 1992, and the 51st Fighter Wing on October 1, 1993

BELOW: 80-0251 assigned to the 25th TFS, 51st Composite Wing with OS tail codes was photographed on June 2, 1982, shortly after the aircraft's arrival at Suwon AB, Korea. (Don McGarry)

80-0251 in 25th TFS markings with OS tail codes and full color PACAF and 51st Composite Wing Insignia when photographed on July 16, 1982 at Suwon AB, Korea. (Don McGarry)

112

PACIFIC AIR FORCES

25th Tactical Fighter Squadron (Assam Dragons)

The 25th TFS moved to Suwon AB Korea from 18th TFW, Kadena AB, Okinawa, without personnel or equipment on February 1, 1981. The 25th began receiving its A-10s in January, 1982. The 25th was planned for conversion to F-16, and gave up all its A-10s by November 9, 1989. The 25th borrowed a few F-16s as part of the conversion plans, but was inactivated on July 31, 1990. The 25th again activated, but with OA-10s, on October 1, 1993

The 25th TFS A-10s were all painted in European I camouflage. The original tail code was OS standing for Osan, the location of the wing headquarters. In early 1984 the codes were changed to SU, standing for Suwon. Full-color PACAF insignia were standard on the tail above the tail code. A miniature red lightning bolt was at the top of the tail.

The 25th was activated on October 1, 1993 once again with OA-10s. This was a result of the Air Force's attempt to retain as many of its historically prominent units as possible during downsizing. At the same time the 51st became a Fighter Wing. The Assam Dragons reapplied the OS tail code and added the 51st FW's galloping horse on both sides of the fuselage. The tail caps were green with a yellow lightning bolt. The 25th FS has started to receive A-10s in the new gray camouflage.

80-0246, of the 25th TFS, in European I paint and SU tail codes was photographed during October 1987. A small lightning bolt is painted on the top of the tail. (Craig Kaston)

80-0213 of the 25th TFS, 51st TFW, marked with SU tail codes, was photographed at Nellis in February 1987. (Marty Isham)

CHAPTER 2: A-10 FLYING UNITS

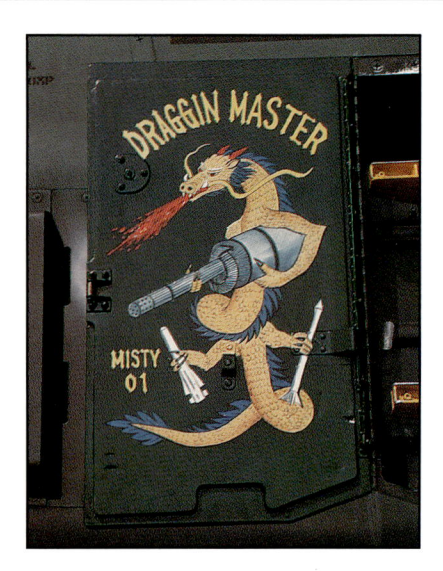

ABOVE: 80-0213, the 25th FS commanders flagship has ladder door art "DRAGGIN MASTER MISTY 01" Misty 01 is the call sign used by the commander. (Alec Fushi)

80-0213, "DRAGGIN MASTER", the 25th FS flagship, 51st Fighter Wing carries the green tail cap with a yellow lightning bolt when photographed in April 1995 at OSAN AB, Korea. (Alec Fushi)

PACIFIC AIR FORCES

80-0163 of the 25th FS, in new gray paint, was photographed in December 1995 at Osan AB, Korea. The A-10A carries the 51st FW's Mustang on the side of the fuselage. (Alec Fushi)

81-0973, of the 25th FS in new gray paint was photographed in December 1995 at Osan AB, Korea. (Alec Fushi)

CHAPTER 2: A-10 FLYING UNITS

80-0243 of the 25th FS photographed on takeoff from Osan AB during April 1995. (Alec Fushi)

78-0685, of the 25th FS, 51st FW, on taxi back with empty TER bomb racks and an ALQ-184(v)-1 long ECM pod, photographed at Osan AB, Korea on April 1995. (Alec Fushi)

80-0241 carrying an AIM-9 Sidewinder missile, empty TER bomb racks, a TGM-65 captive training Maverick, and an AN/AA-35(V)(1) Pave Penny Laser Target Identification pod when photographed at Osan AB, Korea on April 1995 25th FS. (Alec Fushi)

PACIFIC AIR FORCES

ABOVE: 25th FS A-10A 81-0971 photographed on taxi back with empty TER bomb racks, a TGM-65 captive training Maverick, and an ALQ-184(v)-1 long ECM pod at Osan AB during April 1995. (Alec Fushi)

LEFT AND BELOW: 82-0652, with "MIASIS DRAGON II" ladder door art, was photographed at Osan AB, Korea during April 1995. (Alec Fushi)

CHAPTER 2: A-10 FLYING UNITS

RIGHT AND BELOW: 81-0971 with "ELVIS LIVES F.E.S.C." ladder door art, was photographed at Osan AB, Korea during April 1995. (Alec Fushi)

PACIFIC AIR FORCES

19th Tactical Air Support Squadron

The 19th began conversion from OV-10 Broncos to OA-10s, moving to Suwon on August 1, 1989, and replacing the 25th FS. This was a month before the 25th TFS began giving up its A-10s. The 19th TASS assigned to the 5th Tactical Air Control Group (TAIRCG) based at Osan. On October 1, 1990, the 19th TASS moved to Osan and was assigned to the 51st FG. The 19th TASS inactivated on October 1, 1993, being replaced by the newly activated 25th FS.

19th TASS OA-10s were painted in European I camouflage. Several were repainted in PACAF's FAC color scheme of overall 36118 Gunship Gray. SU tail code was carried briefly, changing to OS when the 19th moved to Osan. The 19th TASS tail markings were a variation of the 25th TFS's with a small yellow lightning bolt.

80-0213, of the 19th TASS, painted Gunship Gray with SU tail codes was photographed at Suwon AB, Korea on April 15, 1989. (Kevin Patrick)

80-0243, of the 19th TASS, painted European I with SU tail codes was photographed at Suwon AB, Korea on April 15, 1989. (Kevin Patrick)

CHAPTER 2: A-10 FLYING UNITS

ALASKAN AIR COMMAND

EIELSON AFB, ALASKA
343rd Wing
The 343rd Composite Wing was activated at Eielson AFB on October 1, 1981. The 343rd took control of the 25th TASS with 0-2s at Eielson AFB, and the 18th TFS with F-4Es at Elmendorf. The 343rd was redesignated a TFW on June 8, 1984. The 25th inactivated on September 1, 1989, without ever receiving A-10s. The Alaskan Air Command was redesignated the Eleventh Air Force and assigned to PACAF on August 9, 1990. On July 1, 1991, the 343rd was redesignated the 343rd Wing. The 343rd inactivated on August 20, 1993, and was replaced by the 354th FW.

BELOW: 80-0254, assigned to the 18th TFS, 343rd TFW, the tail markings are outlined in white for GUNSMOKE 89, the tail cap is made up of the 18th TFS Blue Fox markings of a blue stripe with a black fox. A full color Alaskan Air Command insignia was on tail when photographed at Nellis AFB during October 1989. (Alec Fushi)

ALASKAN AIR COMMAND

18th Tactical Fighter Squadron (Blue Foxes)
The 18th TFS moved to Eielson on January 1, 1982, after receiving two A-10s in December, 1981. The 18th gave up their A-10s as the 18th began converting to F-16s in March, 1991. On July 1, 1991 the 18th was redesignated as the 18th FS.

The 18ths A-10s were painted in European I camouflage. The aircraft carried AK tail codes, standing for <u>Alas</u>ka. The 18th's markings were made up of a blue tail cap with a black running fox, and full-color insignia.

CHAPTER 2: A-10 FLYING UNITS

ABOVE: 80-0267 of the 18th TFS, 343rd TFW on landing approach at GUNSMOKE 89, Nellis AFB during October 1989. (Alec Fushi)

RIGHT: 80-0254 of the 18th TFS carried "ARCTIC TERMINATOR" ladder door art when photographed in September 1992. (Ben Knowles)

BELOW: 80-0221 of 18th TFS photographed in June 1989. The AK tail code is outlined in blue, and the tail has a full color Alaskan Air Command insignia on tail. (Ben Knowles)

ALASKAN AIR COMMAND

11th Tactical Air Support Squadron

The 11th TASS was activated at Eielson on July 1, 1991 taking control of A-10s from the 18th FS. The 11th TASS was inactivated on October 1, 1993, having been replaced by the 354th FW and 355 FS on August 20, 1993.

The 11th TASS's A-10s were all in European I camouflage. The A-10s wore AK tail codes and had red tail caps. The unit insignias were subdued black-line insignias.

The tail of 80-0254, the 11th TASS flagship has a red tail cap with a PACAF (Pacific Air Forces) insignia on the tail. (Ben Knowles)

CHAPTER 2: A-10 FLYING UNITS

80-0254, the 11th TASS flagship, photographed in July 1989, has the head of an Alaskan husky as the ladder door art. (Ben Knowles)

80-0240, an OA-10A of the 11th TASS photographed at airshow in September 1992, is marked with a black outline PACAF (Pacific Air Forces) insignia on the tail. (Ben Knowles)

354th Fighter Wing
355th Fighter Squadron (Falcons)

The 354th Fighter Wing activated at Eielson on August 20, 1993, replacing the 343rd Wing and assuming control its personnel and equipment. The 11th TASS inactivated and replaced by the 355th FS also on August 20, 1993.

The 355th retained the 11th TASS markings, changing only the squadron and wing insignias. The first gray OA-10 was painted on base in February, 1994.

80-0259 of the 354th FW, is marked as the 355th FS flagship, It was photographed at McChord AFB, Washington on February 7, 1994, and carries a PACAF (Pacific Air Forces) insignia on the tail. (Renato E.F. Jones)

80-0178 of the 355th FS, 354th FW photographed at Nellis during November, 1995. (David F. Brown)

CHAPTER 2: A-10 FLYING UNITS

U.S. AIR FORCES-EUROPE (USAFE)

RAF BENTWATERS/RAF WOODBRIDGE, ENGLAND
81st Tactical Fighter Wing

In 1978, the 81st TFW became the first USAFE unit to receive A-10s. Stationed at the two bases of RAF Bentwaters and RAF Woodbridge, the 81st maintained a rotational detachments at forward operation locations (FOLs) in Germany. The 81st inactivated in May, 1993, with the drawdown of U.S. forces in Europe.

The first European A-10s carried, like all early A-10s were painted in the MASK-10A "False Canopy Scheme." In 1979, the first aircraft painted in European I camouflaged aircraft flew in from the U.S.

81st Wing aircraft carried WR tail codes. As with other wings, full color insignias and other markings were carried for special events. Squadron tail stripes began to appear in early 1985. Individual squadron designs were later added to the color stripes.

The tail of 81-0981 photographed on July 29, 1988 as the 81th TFW flagship carries the colors of all the wing's squadron: 78th TFS - red; 91st TFS - blue; 92nd TFS - yellow; 509th TFS light gray; 510th TFS magenta; and 511th TFS black. (Kevin Foy)

81-0981 was painted as the 81st TFW flagship when photographed at RAF Bentwaters on July 29, 1988. (Kevin Foy)

81-0952, assigned to the 92nd TFS, carried full color 81st TFW patch and outlined WR tail code with a yellow/black tail stripe when photographed at DM AFB on September 25, 1983. (Brian C. Rogers)

U.S. AIR FORCES-EUROPE (USAFE)

77-0222, in its delivery paint scheme, was photographed at DM in August, 1979 during initial training of the wing's pilots. (Douglas Slowiak Vortex Photo Graphic)

77-0245 in delivery Mask 10A paint scheme on August 27, 1980 at RAF Alconbury. (M. France)

77-0245 photographed in May 1981. The wing and vertical stab tips have been painted in dark green. (Tom Kaminski Collection)

CHAPTER 2: A-10 FLYING UNITS

77-0255 photographed in European I paint scheme during February 1979 at DM AFB. (Ben Knowles)

77-0234 photographed in European I paint scheme during April 13, 1979 at DM AFB. (Brian C. Rogers)

81-0981, the 81st TFW flagship, photographed here at LOADEO 66 weapons loading competition during May 1986. (Tom Kaminski Collection)

U.S. AIR FORCES-EUROPE (USAFE)

78th Tactical Fighter Squadron (Bushmasters)

The 78th TFS received its first A-10s in May, 1979, converting from F-4Ds. The 78th inactivated on May 4, 1992. The squadron stripe was red, and was later changed to red with white borders.

LEFT: 80-0207 is carrying the white bordered red tail stripe of the 78th TFS. (Via Keith Snyder)

80-0270 78th TFS red tail with white Indian head was carried on all 81st TFW A-10s. It was photographed on July 6, 1985 at Nellis AFB. (Pat Martin)

80-0143, a 78th TFS A-10 carrying the squadron's red stripe. The white Indian head has partially worn off. (Tom Kaminski Collection)

CHAPTER 2: A-10 FLYING UNITS

91st Tactical Fighter Squadron (Blue Streaks)

The 91st converted from F-4Ds to A-10s in July, 1979. The 91st inactivated on August 14, 1992. The squadron stripe was blue. White borders and a white lightning bolt were added later.

RIGHT: The 91st TFS blue tail stripe included a white lightning bolt as seen here on the squadron flagship 81-0991, photographed on September 26, 1986. (Kevin Foy)

BELOW: 81-0991, the 91st TFS flagship, was photographed on September 26, 1986. (Kevin Foy)

U.S. AIR FORCES-EUROPE (USAFE)

76-0550 with the 91st TFS blue tail stripe photographed shortly after converting to A-10s in July of 1979. (Tom Kaminski Collection)

81-0951 the 91st TFS also carried the 81st TFW white Indian head on its blue tail stripe. (Tom Kaminski Collection)

As seen on 82-0655, the 91st TFS blue tail stripe remained, with the Indian head being replaced by a white lightning bolt. As seen in this photograph, 82-0655 was fitted with the large GAU-8 muzzle flash deflector. (Tom Kaminski Collection)

131

CHAPTER 2: A-10 FLYING UNITS

92nd Tactical Fighter Squadron
(Skulls)

The 92nd TFS became USAFE's first operational A-10 squadron in January, 1979, after converting from F-4Ds in July, 1978. The 92nd inactivated in March, 1993. The squadron band was yellow, later it was changed to yellow with white borders, and then adding a black skull.

ABOVE: The 92nd TFS added the white Indian head to its yellow tail stripe, 80-281 was photographed at Nellis AFB on July 6.1985 at Nellis AFB. (Pat Martin)

BELOW: 80-0207, with the 92nd TFS yellow tail stripe, photographed shortly after converting to A-10s in July of 1978, wears a full color USAFE insignia. (Tom Kaminski Collection)

As seen on 80-206, the 92nd TFS replaced the white Indian head with black skull on the squadrons yellow tail stripe. 80-206 carried a full color USAFE insignia when photographed at RAF Bentwaters in January 1988. (Kevin Foy)

132

U.S. AIR FORCES-EUROPE (USAFE)

509th Tactical Fighter Squadron (Pirates)

The 509th activated at Bentwaters with A-10s in October, 1979. The 509th moved to the 10th TFW in June, 1988. The squadron stripe was gray, then white borders were added, and finally a black PIRATES and skull was added.

RIGHT: The tail of 81-0947 carried the 509th TFTS tail stripe of light gray with 509th TFS in black when photographed on September 29, 1986. (Kevin Foy)

BELOW: 81-0990 assigned to the 509th TFS, carried a simple light gray tail stripe when photographed on March 21, 1988 at RAF Bentwaters. (Kevin Foy)

CHAPTER 2: A-10 FLYING UNITS

510th Tactical Fighter Squadron (Buzzards)

The 510th TFS activated at Bentwaters on October 1, 1978, and becoming the 81st's second operational A-10 squadron. The 510th ceased operations in December, 1992, and moved to the 52nd FW as the 510th FS in January, 1993. The squadron tail stripe was magenta, later with white borders, a white buzzard's head was later added.

BELOW: 80-0160 carried the 510th TFS magenta stripe with white Buzzard head when photographed in 510th TFS flagship markings at RAF Bentwaters on July 26, 1988. (Kevin Foy)

The 510th TFS also carried the Indian head of the 81st TFW on its magenta stripe as seen on 81-0966 photographed at Nellis AFB on July 6, 1985. (Pat Martin)

U.S. AIR FORCES-EUROPE (USAFE)

511th Tactical Fighter Squadron (Vultures)

The 511th TFS activated at RAF Bentwaters with A-10s on January 1, 1980. The 511th transferred to the 10th TFW at Alconbury in August, 1988. The squadron band was black, which later had white borders and VULTURES in white.

Seen here on July 23, 1987, 81-0955's left vertical stabilizer is marked as the 511th TFS flagship with the squadrons black tail stripe containing "VULTURES" in white. (Pete Wilson)

81-0955's Right vertical stabilizer is marked as the 511th AMU (Aircraft Maintenance Unit)flagship. (Don Logan Collection)

CHAPTER 2: A-10 FLYING UNITS

The 511th TFS black stripe carried the 81st TFW white Indian head when photographed on 80-0275 at Nellis AFB, on July 6, 1985. (Pat Martin)

80-0237 photographed at RAF Bentwaters during August 1988 carried the 511th TFS VULTURES black stripe with white edged black tail letters. (Kevin Foy)

U.S. AIR FORCES-EUROPE (USAFE)

RAF ALCONBURY, ENGLAND

10th Tactical Fighter Wing

The 10th Tactical Reconnaissance Wing gave up their RF-4Cs and was redesignated the 10th TFW in August, 1987. The 10th TFW received two squadrons of A-10s, the 509th FS and the 511th FS, from the 81st TFW a year later. After losing both A-10 squadrons in December, 1992, the 10th remained at Alconbury, redesignated as the 10th Air Base Wing (ABW) on March 31, 1993. The 10th ABW was later inactivated at RAF Alconbury and activated at the U.S. Air Force Academy.

The 10th TFW's A-10s wore European I camouflage with AR Tail code, standing for Alconbury Recon. Squadron tail bands were carried until the summer of 1991.

81-0979, the 10th TFW flagship carried an AR tail code and nose art of a Eagle carrying a submachine gun. (Craig Kaston Collection)

CHAPTER 2: A-10 FLYING UNITS

509th Tactical Fighter Squadron (Pirates)

The 509th TFS moved from RAF Upper Heyford to RAF Alconbury in June, 1988. The 509th ceased operations on December 18, 1991, and was inactivated. The gray squadron tail band originally allied while the 509th was part of the 81st TFW was retained. The PIRATES script in the stripe was later replaced by the squadron insignia.

BELOW: 77-0241 photographed carrying the 509th TFS gray tail stripe at RAF Bentwaters on February 14, 1991. (Don Logan Collection)

81-0987 carried the 509th TFS gray tail stripe and white skull emblem of the PIRATES when photographed at RAF Bentwaters on March 18, 1990. (Don Logan Collection)

80-0220 photographed with the 509th TFS gray tail stripe. (Don Logan Collection)

U.S. AIR FORCES-EUROPE (USAFE)

511th Tactical Fighter Squadron (Vultures)

The 511th moved from RAF Upper Heyford and transferred to the 10th TFW in August, 1988. The 511th ceased operations on March 27, 1992, remaining a paper organization until its inactivation on December 18, 1992. The squadron tail band was black with white borders and Vultures in white script.

LEFT: 82-0659 carries the 511th TFS Vultures tail stripe it wore while assigned to the 10th TFW at RAF Alconbury. The photograph was taken at AMARC, DM AFB Arizona during September, 1989. (Tom Kaminski Collection)

80-0275 of the 511th TFS Vultures, 10th TFW, RAF Alconbury, photographed in July 1988 at RAF Bentwaters. (Kevin Foy)

77-0259, in 511th TFS markings waiting at "last chance" prior to takeoff on a training mission. (Via Keith Snyder)

139

CHAPTER 2: A-10 FLYING UNITS

SPANGDHALEM AB, GERMANY

52nd Fighter Wing
81st Fighter Squadron

In January, 1993, the 510th FS moved its A-10s to Spangdhalem AB, Germany from the 81st TFW at RAF Upper Heyford. The 510th was inactivated on February 1, 1994 with the A-10s transferring to the reorganized 81st FS on February 25, 1994. The 81st FS, having been an F-4G Wild Weasel squadron, sent its aircraft back to the U.S. The 510th FS moved (minus personnel and equipment) to Aviano, Italy, and was activated on July 1, 1994 flying F-16C/Ds. Spangdhalem's A-10, the 81st FS, became the last A-10 unit based in Europe.

All 510th A-10s at Spangdhalem AB were painted in a version of the Ghost Grays camouflage, but did not have the false canopy. They carried the standard Spangdhalem SP tail code (standing for Spangdhalem) tail code as the only unit-applied markings. The 81st FS present markings are black fin caps with white lightning bolts.

81-0952, the 52nd Fighter Wing flagship photographed at Shaw AFB during October 1995 carries the squadron colors of the wing's four squadrons at the time; the 22nd FS - red flying F-16C/D, the 23rd FS - blue flying F-16C/D, the 53rd FS - yellow flying F-15C/D, and the 81st FS - black flying A-10A/OA-10A. (Norm Taylor)

81-0952, the 52nd Fighter Wing flagship, photographed on takeoff at DM AFB during September 1995. (Ben Knowles)

81-0952, the 52nd Fighter Wing flagship, photographed at Shaw AFB during October 1995. (Norm Taylor)

U.S. AIR FORCES-EUROPE (USAFE)

81-0980, 81st FS flagship, photographed at Aviano AB in August, 1996 is carrying an AIM-9 sidewinder and an AGM-65 Maverick under the right wing. (Alec Fushi)

This shot of the left side of the 81st FS flagship, 81-0980, was also photographed at Aviano AB during August 1996. (Alec Fushi)

81-0966 an 81st FS A-10 was photographed at Aviano AB in August 1996, deployed from Spangdalem AB in support of air operations over Bosnia. (Alec Fushi)

CHAPTER 2: A-10 FLYING UNITS

81-0984 of the 81st FS, 52nd Fighter Wing, photographed on landing at DM AFB on March 10, 1995. (Don Logan)

81-0962 of the 81st FS, 52nd Fighter Wing photographed at DM AFB on March 10, 1995. (Don Logan)

81-0954 of the 510th FS, 52nd Fighter Wing photographed on September, 1993 carries the black tail cap with a white lightning bolt later carried by the 81st FS. (Jerry Geer)

U.S. AIR FORCES-EUROPE (USAFE)

LEFT: 81st FS tail markings seen here on 81-0984 consist of a black tail cap with a white lightning bolt on the outside of each vertical stabilizer. (Don Logan)

81-0962 and 81-0984 of the 81st FS, 52nd Fighter Wing were photographed at DM AFB on March 10, 1995. (Don Logan)

81-0985, of the 52nd Fighter Wing, photographed at Shaw AFB during October 1995. (Norm Taylor)

CHAPTER 2: A-10 FLYING UNITS

AIR FORCE RESERVE

BARKSDALE AFB, LOUISIANA
917th Wing

The 917 Tactical Fighter Group, AFRES, at Barksdale AFB received their first A-10s in June, 1980. They were assigned to the 47th TFS and were the first front line aircraft ever delivered direct from the factory to an AFRES unit. The 917th TFG was then a part of the 434th TFW at Grissom AFB, Indiana. The 917th was redesignated as a Tactical Fighter Wing in 1988 when the 926th TFG at New Orleans was assigned. All units dropped the word Tactical from their designations on June 1, 1992. The 93rd BS activated with B-52s, replacing of the 46th FTS, giving the redesignated 917th Wing a strategic bomber capability, a capability never before possessed by the Air Force Reserves.

On October 1, 1996, the 917th Wing once again began training A-10 pilots with the 47th FS augmenting the 355th Wing at Davis-Monthan AFB. The 47th FS is programmed to train 43 Air National Guard and Air Force Reserve A-10 pilots each year.

A-10s of the 917th were all delivered in European I camouflage, but have since been repainted to the new ghost grays. They carry BD (Barksdale) tail codes. The 47th's original markings were metallic green tail tops. When the 46th activated, the tail caps of their aircraft were painted metallic blue. Aircraft of the two squadrons were divided between four maintenance flights. The flights used black, silver, gold, and red as flight colors. The squadron colored tail caps were used in combination with the flight colored tail stripe in the following combinations:

Two experimental paint schemes; "Flipper" the aircraft in the foreground and "Peanut" next to it on the 917th Tactical Fighter Wing ramp at Barksdale AFB Louisiana, were applied by the 917th TFW during mid-1991. (Dana Bell)

144

AIR FORCE RESERVE

46th TFTS/FTS,
- A Flight Blue Cap with Black Border
- B Flight Blue Cap with Silver Border
- C Flight Blue Cap with Gold Border
- D Flight Blue Cap with Red Border

47th TFS
- A Flight Green with Black border
- B Flight Green with Silver border

Since June, 1994, when Brig. Gen. Bill Lawson assumed command of the 917th Wing, the unit's A-10s have carried a metallic green and blue checkerboard fin cap.

The Barksdale A-10s carry the fearsome warthog face painted on the nose of each aircraft. With the trend to tone down the markings on combat aircraft, the white teeth and tusks first used on this marking made the aircraft too visible and were replaced by a subdued warthog nose by November, 1985. One aircraft (79-0148) presently has the non-subdued black and white marking.

The 917th TFW's first Hog's head was airbrushed and more colorful than the later faces which used more subdued colors. (Don Logan Collection)

The 917th was the first to paint Hog's heads on their A-10s. 79-0147 photographed on September 24, 1982 carries the 917th first version of the hogs head. (Doug Remington)

CHAPTER 2: A-10 FLYING UNITS

79-0153, the 917th Wing Commanders aircraft photographed at Barksdale AFB in May 1995, carries a command stripe of green, blue, and gold. Green and blue are the squadron colors for the 47th FS, and blue and gold are the colors of the wing's other squadron, the 93rd Bomb Squadron flying B-52H's. The A-10 also carries the 917th Wing's hogs head on the nose in subdued grays. (Don Logan)

79-0148 differs from the other A-10s of the 47th FS in that it carries a hogs head in black and white, instead of the subdued colors of the unit's other A-10s. (Don Logan)

Photographed during May, 1995, 79-0149 was one of the units last European I painted A-10s, all have since been painted in the new light grays. (Don Logan)

AIR FORCE RESERVE

46th Tactical Fighter Training Squadron

On October 1, 1983, the 46th Tactical Fighter Training Squadron was activated as part of the 917th TFG. The 46th Tactical Fighter Training Squadron became the 46th Fighter Training Squadron on June 1, 1992. The 46th FTS inactivated on October 1, 1993 and was replaced by the 93rd Bomb Squadron flying B-52Hs, passing the training of Reserve Warthog pilots the 355th Wing at Davis-Monthan AFB.

LEFT: 79-0146 was the 46th Tactical Fighter Training Squadron (TFTS) flagship when photographed in May 1990. It carries the blue and silver tail cap of the 46 TFTS, B flight. (Ben Knowles)

79-0146, the 46th TFTS flagship was photographed in May 1990 during a deployment to DM AFB. (Ben Knowles)

79-0105, a member of B flight, 46th TFS, as evidenced by the blue and silver tail cap, carried a green hogs head airbrushed on its nose. (Ray Leader)

147

CHAPTER 2: A-10 FLYING UNITS

78-0701 as a member of C Flight, 46th TFTS, had blue and gold tail caps. (Ben Knowles)

76-0624, a member of C flight, 46th TFTS, as evidenced by the blue and gold tail cap, was photographed in May 1990 during a deployment to DM AFB. (Ben Knowles)

78-0657, also a member of C flight, 46th TFTS, was photographed in November 1990. (Ben Knowles)

148

AIR FORCE RESERVE

LEFT: 76-0519 carries the blue and black tail cap of A flight, 46th TFTS. (Ben Knowles)

76-0519, a member of A flight, 46th TFTS, as evidenced by the blue and black tail cap, was photographed in May 1990 during a deployment to DM AFB. (Ben Knowles)

78-0582 carried the blue and red tail of 46th TFTS D flight when photographed at McConnell AFB, Kansas in September, 1988. (Don Logan)

CHAPTER 2: A-10 FLYING UNITS

47th Fighter Squadron

The 47th Tactical Fighter Squadron, AFRES, received their first A-10s in June, 1980, delivered direct from the factory to AFRES. The 47th TFS became the 47th Fighter Squadron (FS) on June 1, 1992. They again assumed the pilot training mission for AFRES and ANG A-10s on October 1, 1996.

79-0147 was the 47th Tactical Fighter Squadron (TFS) flagship when photographed in May 1990. It carries the green and black tail cap of the 47 TFS, A flight. (Ben Knowles)

BELOW: 79-0147, the 47th TFS flagship was photographed in May 1990 during a deployment to DM. The 46th TFS insignia is painted on the ladder door. (Ben Knowles)

79-0147 was still marked as the 47th Fighter Squadron flagship when photographed at Barksdale AFB on September 26, 1993. (Don Logan)

79-0147 was one of the last of the 917th's A-10 in European I, still marked as the 47th FS flagship, but with the new checked tail cap when photographed at Barksdale AFB in May, 1995. (Don Logan)

78-0582, in the new gray paint carries the green and blue checked tail cap of the 47th FS. (Don Logan)

The tail cap markings of the 47th FS were changed to green and blue checks during late 1994 as evidenced by this photo of 79-0147's tail taken on May, 1995. (Don Logan)

78-0582, like all the other 917th Wing A-10s is painted in the new ghost gray camouflage. (Don Logan)

CHAPTER 2: A-10 FLYING UNITS

This sand and brown "Peanut" camouflage applied to 76-0552, developed just prior to Desert Storm by the 917th Wing was not accepted by the USAF. (Jody Louviere)

The "Peanut" camouflaged aircraft (76-0552) also carried the 917th's hog face. (Jody Louviere)

This three gray "Flipper" camouflage on 76-0530, also developed by the 917th Wing, just prior to Desert Storm was also not accepted by the USAF. 77-0205, 77-0227, 77-0268, 77-0269, and 77-0272 were also painted in the flipper scheme. (Jody Louviere)

152

AIR FORCE RESERVE

78-0150 of the 917th Wing AFRES at Barksdale AFB, Louisiana is seen here on the ramp at Aviano AB, Italy during Operation Deny Flight. (917th WG Public Affairs Office)

Some of the 917th's A-10s deployed to Aviano AB, like 79-0095 seen here, were kept in the hardened shelters like this one. (917th WG Public Affairs Office)

79-0105 also deployed to Aviano AB during Operation Deny Flight. (917th WG Public Affairs Office)

CHAPTER 2: A-10 FLYING UNITS

47th Fighter Squadron Lil' Abner Cartoon Art

79-0146 LI'L ABNER. (Don Logan)

79-0142 SALOMEY. (Don Logan)

79-0105 AVAILABLE JONES. (Don Logan)

79-0153 MARRYIN' SAM. (Don Logan)

79-0143 LONSOME POLECAT. (Don Logan)

79-0095 ROMEO SCRAGG. (Don Logan)

79-0094 HONEST ABE YOKUM. (Don Logan)

79-0145 GENERAL BULLMOOSE. (Don Logan)

79-0155 HAIRLESS JOE. (Don Logan)

AIR FORCE RESERVE

GRISSOM AFB, INDIANA

930th Operations Group
45th Fighter Squadron (Hoosier Hogs)

Converting from A-37s, the 434th TFW and its 45th TFS received their first A-10s in June, 1981. In July, 1987, the 434th TFW was reorganized as the 434th Air Refueling Wing. Control of the 45th TFS and their A-10s passed to the newly activated 930th TFG. Tactical was dropped from the unit designations on February 1, 1992. On August 1, 1992, the 930th FG became an operations group (OG), still with the 434th Wing. The 930th OG retired its A-10s on September 30, 1994 and deactivated on October 1, 1994.

Originally all Grissom's A-10s were painted in European I camouflage. The 45th TFS used IN tail codes standing for Indiana. The tail caps were blue bordered on the bottom with black for A Flight or yellow for B Flight. The IN tail code was black edged in light blue. Like other USAF aircraft units based in Indiana, 45th aircraft carried a race car and checkered flag motif (for the Indianapolis Raceway) overlaid on a map of Indiana was located on the tail of each aircraft. In celebration of the 50th anniversary of D-Day an Indiana A-10 was painted with the black and white invasion stripes carried on D-Day by allied aircraft.

77-0245 of the 45th TFS, 434th TFW, AFRES, photographed on takeoff at NAS Glenview in July 1990. (Norris Graser)

80-0276 of the 45th FS, 930th Operations Group, AFRES in ghost gray paint photographed on March 6, 1994. located on the tail of each of the 45th FS A-10s, above the IN tail code is a map of the state of Indiana overlaid with a race car and checkered flags (representing the Indianapolis Raceway). (Norris Graser)

CHAPTER 2: A-10 FLYING UNITS

ABOVE AND BELOW: In May 1994, as part of the celebration of the 50th anniversary of the D-Day invasion, 80-0149 was painted with invasion stripes similar to those carried by the P-47, the first Thunderbolt. (Keith Snyder)

80-0187, photographed on September 18, 1993, with Indiana ANG markings, displays the hogs head of 917th TFW. (Keith Snyder)

AIR FORCE RESERVE

77-0229 of the 45th FS, 930th Operations Group (OG), AFRES in European I camouflage photographed on July 27, 1992. The yellow border on the blue tail cap indicates the aircraft belonged to B flight. (Norris Graser)

77-0217 photographed on February 3, 1992, two days after the 45th FS passed to the 930th OG. The black border on the blue tail cap indicates the aircraft belonged to A flight. (Norris Graser)

CHAPTER 2: A-10 FLYING UNITS

NAS NEW ORLEANS, LOUISIANA

926th Fighter Wing
706th Fighter Squadron (Cajuns)

The 706th TFS, 926th TFG, at NAS New Orleans, Louisiana, received its first A-10s in December, 1981, completing the conversion form A-37s in June, 1982. The group was initially assigned to the 434th TFW at Grissom, transferring to the 442nd TFW at Richards-Gebaur on February 1, 1984. On July 1, 1987 it transferred to the 917th TFW at Barksdale on July 1, 1987. The 926th was activated for Desert Shield/Desert Storm on December 29, 1990 and deployed eighteen aircraft, including one loaned from the 47th TFS at Barksdale. The group was released from active duty on June 15, 1991. On February 1, 1992, the units Tactical from their designations. The group transitioned to F-16s in October, 1992, sending many of their A-10s to AMARC for storage.

On May 22, 1996, the 706th FS began their conversion back to the A-10 with the receipt of 78-0655 and 80-0237 from the 20th Fighter Wing at Shaw AFB. The 47th FS at Barksdale provided 79-0106 and 79-0136 on June 17, 1996. 79-0093, 79-0121, and 80-0188 came from the 442nd FW, AFRES, at Whiteman AFB, Missouri. The 926th Fighter Wing finished their transition back to the A-10 with the official welcoming ceremony held on October 18, 1996.

RIGHT: 77-0269 seen here with Belle Of New Orleans nose art. (Jody Louviere)

BELOW: 77-0269 carried markings as the Belle Of New Orleans during Desert Storm. The 706th TFS marked the aircraft's kills on a scoreboard on the right side of the nose. (Kevin Foy)

AIR FORCE RESERVE

The 926th's tail code was NO derived from New Orleans. Tail caps were painted red with flight color borders of black for A Flight or white for B Flight added in 1985. The group's A-10s carried nose art and/or nicknames during and after Desert Storm, in fact most carried the nose art all the way to AMARC.

The 926th Fighter Wing new markings are similar to those previously applied to their F-16s. The A-10 tail carries the same NO as before. In keeping with the 926th's use of the New Orleans motif and Mardi Gras colors, the new tail stripe is purple and green with yellow fleurs-de-lis painted in the purple portion of the stripe. AFRES has been applied to the engine nacelles.

77-0260 carried nose art of a four leaf clover during Desert Storm. (Jody Louviere)

77-0271, carried the nose art HOLY *#—+! and DESERT STORM 91 on the nose. (Jody Louviere)

CHAPTER 2: A-10 FLYING UNITS

ABOVE: 77-0267 with the 706th FS red tail cap was photographed at Bradley International Airport, Windsor Locks, Connecticut on September 1, 1991. (Gilles Auliard)

RIGHT: A-10 79-0106 tail shows the colors of the new 706th markings. (Nate Leong)

All of the 706th Squadron's new A-10s are painted in the new two gray camouflage like 79-0106 seen here at NAS New Orleans on October 18, 1996. (Nate Leong)

80-0188 shortly after its arrival from the 442nd FW at Whiteman AFB wearing only the NO tail code of the 706th FS. (Nate Leong)

160

AIR FORCE RESERVE

WHITEMAN AFB, MISSOURI

442nd Fighter Wing
303rd Fighter Squadron (KC Hawgs)

In October, 1982, the 442nd Tactical Airlift Wing based at Richards-Gebaur AFB, outside Kansas City, Missouri gave up its C-130Es and became the 442nd TFG as the 303rd TFS began converting to A-10s. The 442nd TFG was redesignated as the 442nd TFW in February, 1984. Tactical was dropped from unit designations on February 1, 1992. With the closing of Richards-Gebaur, on June 11 and 12, 1994, the wing moved to Whiteman AFB, Missouri.

A-10s of the 442nd were delivered in standard European I camouflage, with the A-10s in the new grays beginning to arrive in 1993. The aircraft carried KC tail codes standing for Kansas City. The tail caps on the European I aircraft were black with a gold bottom border. The new gray camouflage aircraft did not have the tail caps painted black, but did retain the gold line which had been the border. With the move to Whiteman, the 442nd 's markings remained unchanged.

This front view of 79-0177 on the ramp at Richards-Gebaur AFB, Missouri shows the offset nose gear, which allows the gun to be mounted on the centerline. (Don Logan)

CHAPTER 2: A-10 FLYING UNITS

79-0110 prepares to taxi out after a stopover at DM AFB on March 21, 1983. (Brian C. Rogers)

The 442nd TFG, 303rd TFS markings consisted of a black tail cap with a yellow stripe on the bottom, and the tail code KC. The KC stood for Kansas City, the 442nd TFG's home, Richards-Gebaur AFB was located 17 miles south of Kansas City, Missouri. In addition, 78-0631, seen here was photographed at DM AFB on February 4, 1983, has an extra black stripe on its wing tip. (Brian C. Rogers)

79-0121 was photographed on a stopover at Luke AFB during March, 1993. Barely visible on the engine nacelle is AFRES. (Douglas E. Slowiak Vortex Photo Graphics)

AIR FORCE RESERVE

78-0631 of the 442 Fighter Wing, AFRES, was photographed at Volk Field during July of 1992. (Norris Graser)

80-0123 was photographed on takeoff at DM during March 1995. (Ben Knowles)

80-0201 was photographed on the 917th Wing ramp at Barksdale AFB on May 25, 1995, after completing a night vision goggle modification accomplished there. The unit's aircraft no longer are painted with the black tail cap. (Don Logan)

CHAPTER 2: A-10 FLYING UNITS

80-0188, photographed on the ramp at Aviano AB, Italy during Operation Deny Flight. The A-10's of the 442nd FG use a non standard script type for their tail code and serial numbers. (917th WG Public Affairs Office)

ABOVE AND BELOW: 79-0114, at Aviano is carrying a Maverick, target marking rockets, and an ALQ-131 (deep) ECM pod under the left wing. (917th WG Public Affairs Office)

AIR NATIONAL GUARD

BRADLEY ANGB, CONNECTICUT ANG
103rd Fighter Wing
118th Fighter Squadron (The Flying Yankees)

The 103rd TFG, 118th TFS (Flying Yankees) began converting from F-100s to A-10s at Bradley ANG Base, Windsor Locks, Connecticut, in the summer of 1979. The 103rd became the first ANG unit to fly A-10s, and the first ANG unit to receive new tactical aircraft directly from the factory. Connecticut Air Guard units dropped Tactical from their unit designations on March 16, 1992, with the 103rd FG being redesignated as the 103rd Fighter Wing in 1996.

The 103rd's A-10s were all delivered from the factory in European I camouflage. Unit markings started out simple with black CT tail codes (standing for Connecticut). The 103rd insignia was first carried on the left fuselage above the strake, then moved to the left engine nacelle. Flying Yankees script was later added to the nacelle above the insignia. The ANG insignia was carried on the right side of the fuselage above the strake.

The units new tail markings appeared in 1995 and consisted of a black lightning bolt underlined with a blue stripe and topped by a yellow stripe. The nacelle markings were retained.

81-0965 tail markings. (Tom Kaminski)

CHAPTER 2: A-10 FLYING UNITS

81-0960, of the 103rd at Bradley ANGB on December 4, 1995, displays red, white, and blue Outstanding Unit Award, with its two oak leaf clusters, above and in front of the wing on the right fuselage side. (Tom Kaminski)

RIGHT: The engine nacelles of 81-0965 display nickname and insignia of the 103rd Fighter group. This marking is common to all their aircraft. (Tom Kaminski)

AIR NATIONAL GUARD

78-0641 photographed during September, 1986 shows the highlighted tail codes and on the nacelle, the ANG crest in subdued colors. (Jim Goodall)

78-0619 shows the highlighted tail codes and the 103rd TFG insignia on the nacelle in subdued colors, when photographed during September, 1986. (Jim Goodall)

78-0584 of the 118th TFS, 103rd TFG, Connecticut Air National Guard, is photographed taxiing back to parking space after landing at DM AFB on January 5, 1980. (Brian C. Rogers)

CHAPTER 2: A-10 FLYING UNITS

78-0635, photographed at DM AFB on January 5, 1980, shows the fuselage side location of the National Guard insignia used on early 103rd TFG A-10s. (Brian C. Rogers)

78-0643, photographed at Volk Field, Wisconsin on June 4, 1991 during a practice deployment training exercise. (Norris Graser)

81-0965 photographed at Bradley ANGB during May, 1994. (Paul Hart)

168

AIR NATIONAL GUARD

79-0084, photographed at Bradley ANGB in August, 1994, carries the colors of the 103rd TFG as a blue tail cap with a yellow stripe. (Tom Kaminski)

78-0584's nacelle was still marked for the unit's 70th anniversary (1923 to 1993) when photographed at Bradley ANGB on December 4, 1995. (Tom Kaminski)

82-0646 at Shaw AFB during September 1995 carrying external fuel tanks. (Norm Taylor)

CHAPTER 2: A-10 FLYING UNITS

GOWEN FIELD, IDAHO ANG
124th Wing
190th Fighter Squadron

The 190th Fighter Squadron, 124th Wing, Idaho Air National Guard, located at Gowen Field, Boise Air Terminal, outside Boise, Idaho began converting to the A-10 when their first aircraft arrived from the Massachusetts Air National Guard on March 20, 1996. The 190th sent their last F-4, (the last combat F-4 in the U.S. military), an F-4G Wild Weasel to AMARC at Davis-Monthan on April 20, 1996. Local area training in the A-10 began in August of 1996, with an operational commitment to begin in October, 1997.

Conversion to C-130s for the Airlift Squadron occurred at the same time, making the 124th Wing a two flying squadron wing with an A-10 squadron and a C-130 squadron.

The 190th markings consist of an ID (Idaho) tail code and a white tail cap edged in red with two mountain peaks and IDAHO in blue.

80-0191, an ex Massachusetts ANG A-10 wearing an ID tail code, photographed at the end of May, 1996, on the ramp at Barnes Field ANGB, awaiting departure for its transfer to the Idaho ANG at Gowen Field, Idaho. (Tim Doherty)

81-0955, an ex 111th FW A-10 at Gowen Field, Idaho, still has its Pennsylvania ANG engine inlet covers. (Tony Sacketos)

78-0611 when photographed in July 1996 carried an ID tail code. Additional markings had not yet been added. (Ben Knowles)

AIR NATIONAL GUARD

WARFIELD ANGB, MARYLAND ANG
175th Wing
104th Fighter Squadron

The 104th TFS, 175th TFG, accepted its first A-10 in October, 1979 replacing A-37s. The 104th received the first LASTE modified A-10s in the ANG. Tactical was dropped from unit designations in March, 1992.

The 175th A-10s were delivered painted in European I camouflage. The aircraft carry MD tail codes, standing for Maryland. The aircraft carried a black outline ANG insignia over the right fuselage strake, and a black outline 175th insignia over the left strake. In late 1985 the markings were revised. The ANG insignia was removed, full color group insignia was applied to the left engine nacelle, and a full-color squadron insignia was placed on the right nacelle. In early 1987, a new MARYLAND band, including flight colors, was added to the tails, and flight colors were revised:

- A Flight - yellow
- B Flight - orange
- C Flight - blue.
- D Flight - green (added in 1993)

The units Europe I painted aircraft have been repainted to the gray scheme retaining their MD tail code, but no longer have tail fin stripes.

79-0175, the 175th FG flagship was photographed on June 9, 1993 at Langley AFB with GUNSMOKE 91 WORLD CHAMPS flanking the Outstanding Unit Citation. (Brian C. Rogers)

CHAPTER 2: A-10 FLYING UNITS

The nacelle markings on 79-0087, photographed in April 1982, commemorate the units deployment to its forward operating location in what was then West Germany. (Jim Goodall)

78-0637, photographed on July 8, 1993 with the white and yellow tail stripe of A flight. (Tom Kaminski)

AIR NATIONAL GUARD

104th TFS/FS Insignia. (Paul Hart)

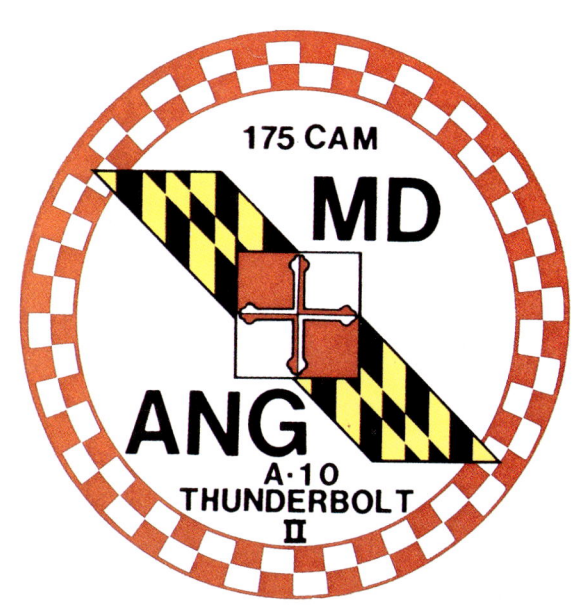

78-0704, photographed during October, 1991 with the orange and white tail stripe of B flight. (Don Logan Collection)

78-0694 photographed during on July 6, 1995 with the Blue and white tail stripe of C flight. (Tom Kaminski)

CHAPTER 2: A-10 FLYING UNITS

During August 1989 the 175th deployed to Wisconsin as part of CENTURY INDEPENDENCE 89. The 175th's A-10 all carried nose art for this deployment. This line up photographed on August 18, 1989, at Madison is made up of, left to right, 78-0627 "Darling Denise", 78-0682 "Mama CAS", 79-0087 "Miss Piggy", 78-0718 "My Barb", 78-0683 "Norris the Playhog", and 78-0693 "Lil' Denise, Iron Maden." (Alec Fushi)

78-0718 "Cleared Hot" photographed August 18, 1989 at Madison, Wisconsin. (Norris Graser)

78-0683 "Norris The Playhog" photographed August 18, 1989 at Madison, Wisconsin. (Norris Graser)

174

AIR NATIONAL GUARD

78-0627 "Darling Denise" photographed August 18, 1989 at Madison, Wisconsin. (Norris Graser)

79-0087 "Miss Piggy" photographed August 18, 1989 at Madison, Wisconsin. (Norris Graser)

78-0682 "Mama CAS" photographed August 18, 1989 at Madison, Wisconsin. (Norris Graser)

CHAPTER 2: A-10 FLYING UNITS

78-0634 photographed on the end of a line of 175th FG A-10s on July 6, 1995. (Tom Kaminski)

78-0702, photographed during December 1994, after recent repaint in the new gray scheme. (Paul Hart)

AIR NATIONAL GUARD

104th Fighter Group ladder door art on 79-0104, the Group flagship. (Tom Kaminski)

BARNES ANGB, MASSACHUSETTS ANG
104th Fighter Wing
131st Fighter Squadron (Death Vipers)

The Massachusetts Air Guard converted to A-10s in July, 1979. The 131st TFS of the 104th TFG is based at Barnes Municipal Airport, near Westfield, Massachusetts. These units were redesignated the 131st FS and 104th FG in March, 1992. Long rumored to be on the F-16 conversion list, the 104th will remain in A-10s through the end of the decade. The 104th Fighter Group was redesignated as the 104th Fighter Wing during early 1996.

All of the 104th's A-10s arrived in European I camouflage. A black MA tail code standing for <u>MA</u>ssachusetts was added. A red tail stripe with five white stars and a black stripe was added by mid-1981. A map of Massachusetts was added to each nacelle in black. A 104 shows through the eastern part of the map in the background camouflage color. The map had been removed by the late 1980s. A full-color Outstanding Unit Citation (with 2 oak leaves) was added to each side of the fuselage above the strakes in 1989. The 104th's A-10 are now painted in the new grays and still carry the 104th's red stripe with five white stars in a + pattern, three stars in the stripe with one star above and one star below the center star in the stripe.

LEFT: 79-0104 marked as the 104th FG flagship displays the Massachusetts Air National Guard tail markings made up of a red stripe with a black stripe and five white stars. (Tim Doherty)

BELOW: 79-0104 "City of Westfield", the 104th TFG flagship with full color markings photographed during July, 1992. (Ben Knowles)

CHAPTER 2: A-10 FLYING UNITS

79-0104, "City of Westfield" photographed on November 4, 1991, with full color 104th TFG and 131st TFS "Vipers" insignia on the engine nacelle. (Norris Graser)

The nacelles on 78-0612, seen here, were marked with the Massachusetts map and "104." (Doug Remington via Tom Brewer)

178

AIR NATIONAL GUARD

78-0617 in European I with full color markings photographed during September 1990. (Ben Knowles)

78-0628 in new gray paint scheme during December 1994. (Gilles Auliard)

78-0659 in new gray at Barnes ANGB, Massachusetts photographed in October 1995. (Paul Hart)

CHAPTER 2: A-10 FLYING UNITS

78-0104, ex "City of Westfield" in new gray paint photographed on December 4, 1995. (Tom Kaminski)

LEFT: DEATH FROM ABOVE ladder door art was painted on 78-0614 when photographed on December 4, 1995. (Paul Hart) RIGHT: "THE EQUALIZER" was the ladder door art painted on 78-0629 when photographed on December 4, 1995. (Tom Kaminski)

78-0616, photographed on December 4, 1995, at Barnes ANGB, carries two bombs as mission markings from the unit's deployment to Bosnia between August 6 and October 16, 1995. (Tom Kaminski)

180

AIR NATIONAL GUARD

78-0640, photographed on December 4, 1995, at Barnes ANGB, carries two bombs as mission markings from the unit's deployment to Bosnia. (Tom Kaminski)

Close up of 78-0640 shows the mission marks above the armament box on the fuselage side. (Tom Kaminski)

Close up of the mission markings on 78-0647 shows one bomb (mission) and a building with a picket fence in front of it. (Tom Kaminski)

CHAPTER 2: A-10 FLYING UNITS

W. K. KELLOGG AIRPORT, MICHIGAN ANG
110th Fighter Wing
172nd Fighter Squadron

The 172nd Tactical Air Support Squadron, 110th Tactical Air Support Group, based at W. K. Kellogg Airport in Battle Creek, Michigan, received its A-10s on October 1, 1991, converting from OA-37s. The units were redesignated the 110th Fighter Group and 172nd Fighter Squadron in March, 1992, with the 110th FG being redesignated as the 110th Fighter Wing in 1996.

All 110th aircraft were received in European I camouflage with the first aircraft repainted to the new Ghost Grays in 1992. The BC tail codes stand for Battle Creek. Initially the tail cap was blue with Michigan in yellow script. Aircraft in the Ghost Grays apply only a black script Michigan to the tail cap, but have applied Battle Creek in script and a map of Michigan to both nacelles.

(Norris Graser)

The 110th FW flagship, 80-0265, photographed taxiing back from a mission at Volk Field on May 15, 1996. (Norris Graser)

80-0265 was marked as the 110th Fighter Wing flagship when photographed at Volk Field, Wisconsin on May 15, 1996. (Norris Graser)

AIR NATIONAL GUARD

RIGHT: 110th Fighter Group tail and nacelle markings were photographed 81-0996 at DM AFB during May, 1995. (Ben Knowles)

BELOW: 81-0996 photographed in June, 1991 has white outlined tail letters and light blue MICHIGAN tail cap on its European I paint scheme. (Jody Louviere)

80-0263 shows off the Michigan map on its intake cover while at Willow Grove Air Reserve Base during August, 1994. (Paul Hart)

CHAPTER 2: A-10 FLYING UNITS

80-0221 in European I was photographed at DM AFB during a Snow Birds deployment in April, 1995. (Ben Knowles)

80-0258 in the new gray paint scheme at DM AFB during April, 1995. (Ben Knowles)

80-0267 in European I was photographed at DM AFB during a Snow Birds deployment in April, 1995. (Ben Knowles)

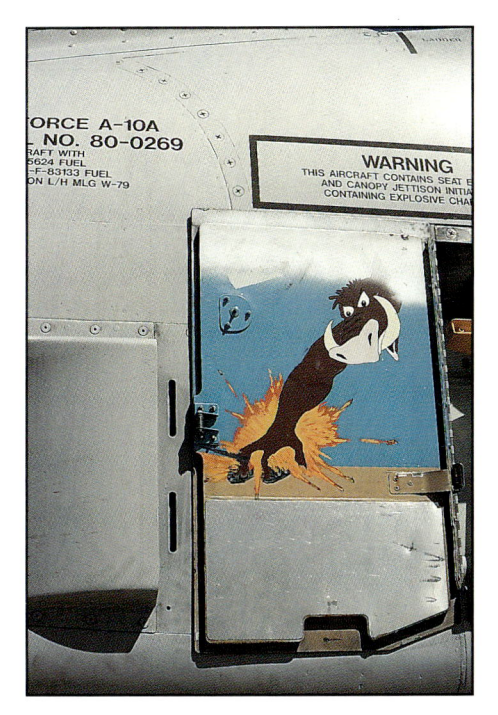

AIR NATIONAL GUARD

80-0269 Ladder Door art on BC A-10s at DM during a Snow Birds deployment. (Ben Knowles)

81-0998 Ladder Door art on BC A-10s at DM during a Snow Birds deployment. (Ben Knowles)

80-0258 Ladder Door art on BC A-10s at DM during a Snow Birds deployment. (Ben Knowles)

80-0267 Ladder Door art on BC A-10s at DM during a Snow Birds deployment. (Ben Knowles)

81-0996 Ladder Door art on BC A-10s at DM during a Snow Birds deployment. (Ben Knowles)

81-0994 Ladder Door art on BC A-10s at DM during a Snow Birds deployment. (Ben Knowles)

CHAPTER 2: A-10 FLYING UNITS

HANCOCK FIELD, NEW YORK ANG
174th Tactical Fighter Wing
138th Tactical Fighter Squadron
(The Boys From Syracuse)

In September, 1979, A-10s officially replaced the A-37s of the 138th Tactical Fighter Squadron, 174th Tactical Fighter Group at Hancock Field, Syracuse, New York. The group was redesignated a Tactical Fighter Wing in October, 1979. In November, 1988, the first F-16s, replacing the A-10s, began arriving at Hancock Field. The last A-10 left in March, 1989.

All of the 174th's A-10s were painted in European I camouflage. The A-10 wore black NY (<u>N</u>ew <u>Y</u>ork) tail codes on the tail, and black gothic lettered "The Boys from Syracuse" painted on each engine nacelle. Each aircraft carried individual artwork inside the ladder door. The 174th kept close ties with its Checkered Flag deployment base in Bavaria and applied special markings to some aircraft in honor of that German state.

78-0670 photographed at Toronto International Airport on September 2, 1985 carried a light blue and white diamond checked command stripe and "BAVARIA" on the right side of the aircraft reflecting ties to its deployment base in the German state of Bavaria. (P. Osborne via Crag Kaston)

78-0670 also photographed during September, 1985 shows the markings and command stripe on the left side of the aircraft. (Tom Kaminski)

AIR NATIONAL GUARD

Markings of the 138th TFS, 174th TFW, were relatively plain consisting of a black NY tail code and "The Boys From Syracuse" in black Gothic script on the engine nacelle as seen on 78-0609 photographed at DM AFB on January 9, 1981. (Brian C. Rogers)

"Thunderbolt Warrior" was the ladder door art carried by 78-0634 when photographed at DM AFB on March 24, 1983. (Brian C. Rogers)

78-0634, photographed at DM AFB with a windshield cover in place on March 24, 1983. (Brian C. Rogers)

CHAPTER 2: A-10 FLYING UNITS

78-0690, "Pigout" photographed on March 24, 1983, at DM AFB. (Brian C. Rogers)

78-0634, Taxiing at Hancock Field, New York during September 1985. (Tom Kaminski)

AIR NATIONAL GUARD

WILLOW GROVE AIR FORCE RESERVE BASE, PENNSYLVANIA ANG
111th Fighter Wing
103rd Fighter Squadron (Black Hogs)

The 103rd Tactical Air Support Squadron, 111th Tactical Air Support Group, at Willow Grove AFRB, Pennsylvania, began converting to OA-10s in 1988. The unit's last OA-37 left in March, 1989. On 16 March, 1992, the units were redesignated the 103rd Fighter Squadron and the 111th Fighter Group. In early 1996 the 111th FG was redesignated as the 111th Fighter Wing in early 1996.

All 111th A-10s were delivered in European I camouflage with repainted Ghost Grays aircraft first appearing in 1992. The black PA tail codes, standing for Pennsylvania. A tail stripe was added in the appropriate maintenance flight color:

    A Flight - yellow
    B Flight - blue
    C Flight - red.

The engine nacelles now carry Pennsylvania Black Hogs in script on both sides. The tail cap marking was changed to black with a red keystone between two white stars.

Pennsylvania map on engine nacelles of the 111th FG flagship 80-0156 on August 15, 1993. (Don Logan)

Tail of the 111th FG Flagship, 80-0156, photographed on August 15, 1993. (Don Logan)

80-0156, "City of Philadelphia" the 111th FW flagship, wearing the "piglets" hog face was photographed at Langley AFB, Virginia on August 15, 1993. (Don Logan)

CHAPTER 2: A-10 FLYING UNITS

82-0659 "Philadelphia Freedom" is the most colorfully marked of the 111th Fighter Wing's aircraft. This series was photographed in July, 1996. (Don Spering/AIR)

AIR NATIONAL GUARD

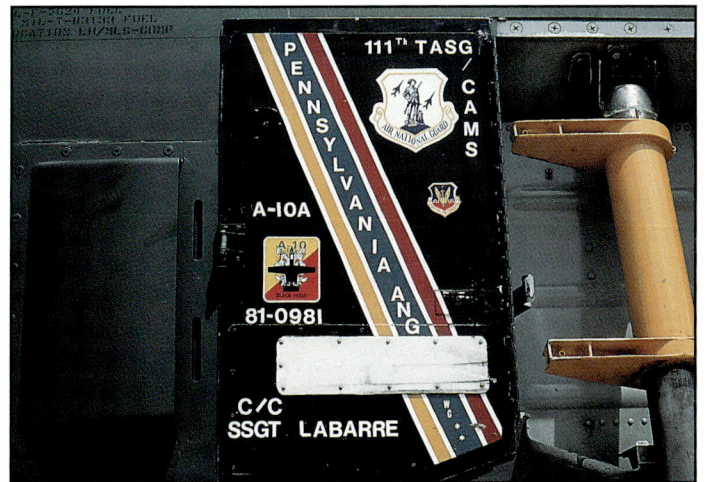

ABOVE: 79-0242 carried a red keystone, derived from Pennsylvania's nickname "The Keystone State", on the nacelle when photographed in June 1990. (David F. Brown)

LEFT: 81-0981's ladder door markings. (Paul Hart)

BELOW: 79-0219 photographed on June 16, 1995 in the 111th's current markings which include "Pennsylvania Black Hogs" on the nacelle and a dark blue tail cap with two white starts and a red keystone. (Paul Hart)

CHAPTER 2: A-10 FLYING UNITS

80-0219 Piglets demonstration team aircraft with the piglets hog face, and a red C flight stripe on the tail. stripe and yellow keystone on the engine inlet cover. (Don Logan Collection)

BELOW: 81-0981 was a member of the Piglets demonstration team, wearing a hog face, and a yellow A flight tail. (Keith Snyder)

80-0227, a member of Piglets demonstration team, wearing a piglets hog face, and a blue B flight stripe and light blue keystone on the engine inlet cover. (Tom Kaminski)

192

AIR NATIONAL GUARD

80-0219, photographed in September 1993, after being repainted in the new gray scheme, still a member Piglets demonstration team, wears the piglets hog face. (Don Logan Collection)

81-0955, photographed in May of 1993 wears the yellow tail cap of A flight. (Tom Kaminski)

During 1994 the tail markings were changed, now made up of a dark blue tail cap with three yellow stars, as photographed on 76-0516 during August, 1994. (Paul Hart)

CHAPTER 2: A-10 FLYING UNITS

81-0949 photographed in September, 1993 with the dark blue B flight tail cap. (Tom Kaminski)

80-0218 was photographed on December 2, 1994, wearing temporary markings with no tail codes and black tail cap with "Pennsylvania" in white script on a dark blue tail cap. (Tom Kaminski)

80-0214 photographed in June 1995 wears a Kangaroo on the bottom of the rudder applied by RAAF personnel during a visit to Australia. (Don Logan Collection)

AIR NATIONAL GUARD

80-0152 carried the red tail cap of C flight when photographed in September, 1993. (Tom Kaminski)

80-0250, photographed on landing at DM AFB February, 1995 wears the new tail cap markings. (Ben Knowles)

79-0219 seen here, photographed on December 2, 1994, with the 111th's new markings of two white stars and red keystone on a dark blue tail cap. (Tom Kaminski)

78-0658, photographed on May 18, 1996 in present markings and European I paint scheme. (Norris Graser)

CHAPTER 2: A-10 FLYING UNITS

TRUAX ANGB, WISCONSIN ANG
128th Fighter Wing
176th Fighter Squadron

The Badger Militia, 176th Tactical Air Support Squadron, 128th Tactical Air Support Wing, officially converted from OA-37s to A-10s on October 1, 1981. That same day, the flying units were redesignated as the 176th TFS and the 128th TFW. On March 16, 1992, Tactical was dropped from the unit designation. The last A-10 left by the end of 1992, being replaced by F-16s.

All 128th A-10s were painted in European I camouflage. The unit's markings in black included WI (Wisconsin) tail code, Outstanding Unit Citation over the fuselage strakes, and the University of Wisconsin "Bucky Badger" in black on each engine nacelle.

BELOW: 78-0690 of the 176th TFS, 128th TFW, on landing approach on June 1992. (Jody Louviere)

77-0246 photographed on February 9, 1983 while taxiing at DM AFB. (Brian C. Rogers)

AIR NATIONAL GUARD

76-0538 photographed at DM AFB on February 7, 1983 wears a WI tail code and Bucky Badger, the mascot of the University of Wisconsin, on the nacelle. (Brian C. Rogers)

CHAPTER 2: A-10 FLYING UNITS

77-0252 photographed at DM AFB on March 20, 1984. (Brian C. Rogers)

77-0262 photographed during June, 1986. (David F. Brown)

A-10 TAIL CODES

AD	3246th Test Wing, Eglin AFB, Florida
AK	343rd WG, Eielson AFB, Alaska
AK	354th FW, Eielson AFB, Alaska
AR	10th TFW, RAF Alconbury, England
BC	110th FG, W.K. Kellogg Airport, Michigan ANG
BD	917th TFG/TFW/WG, AFRES, Barksdale AFB, Louisiana
CT	103rd FG, Bradley ANGB, Connecticut ANG
DM	355th TFW/FW/WG Davis Monthan AFB, Arizona
ED	6510th Test Wing, Edwards AFB, California
ED	412th Test Wing, Edwards AFB, California
EL	23rd TFW, England AFB, Louisiana
ET	3246th Test Wing, Eglin AFB, Florida
FT	23rd WG, Pope AFB, North Carolina
ID	190th FS, 124 WG, Gowen Field, Boise, Idaho ANG
IN	424th TFW, AFRES, Grissom AFB, Indiana
IN	930th TFG/OG, AFRES, Grissom AFB, Indiana
KC	442nd TFG/TFW/FW, AFRES, Whiteman AFB, Missouri
MB	354th TFW/FW Myrtle Beach, South Carolina
MA	104th FG, Barnes ANGB, Massachusetts ANG
MD	175th FG, Warfield ANGB, Maryland ANG
MY	347th WG, Moody AFB, Georgia
NF	602nd ACW Davis-Monthan AFB, Arizona
NO	706 TFS, 926th TFG, AFRES, NAS New Orleans, Louisiana
NY	174th TFW, Hancock Field, New York ANG
OS	51st TFW/FW Osan AB, Korea
OT	4443rd Test and Evaluation Group, Eglin AFB, Florida
OT	57th Test Group, Nellis AFB, Nevada
PA	111th FG, Willow Grove ARB, Pennsylvania ANG
SF	507th ACW, Shaw AFB, South Carolina
SM	2874th Test Squadron/337th Test Squadron, McClellan AFB
SP	52nd FW, Spangdhalem AB, Germany
SU	51st TFW, Suwon AB, Korea
SW	363rd FW, Shaw AFB, South Carolina
SW	20th FW, Shaw AFB, South Carolina
TC	354th FS McChord AFB, Washington
WA	57th FWW/TTW/WG Nellis AFB, Nevada
WI	128th TFW/FW, Truax ANGB, Wisconsin ANG
WR	81st TFW, RAF Bentwaters/RAF Woodbridge, England

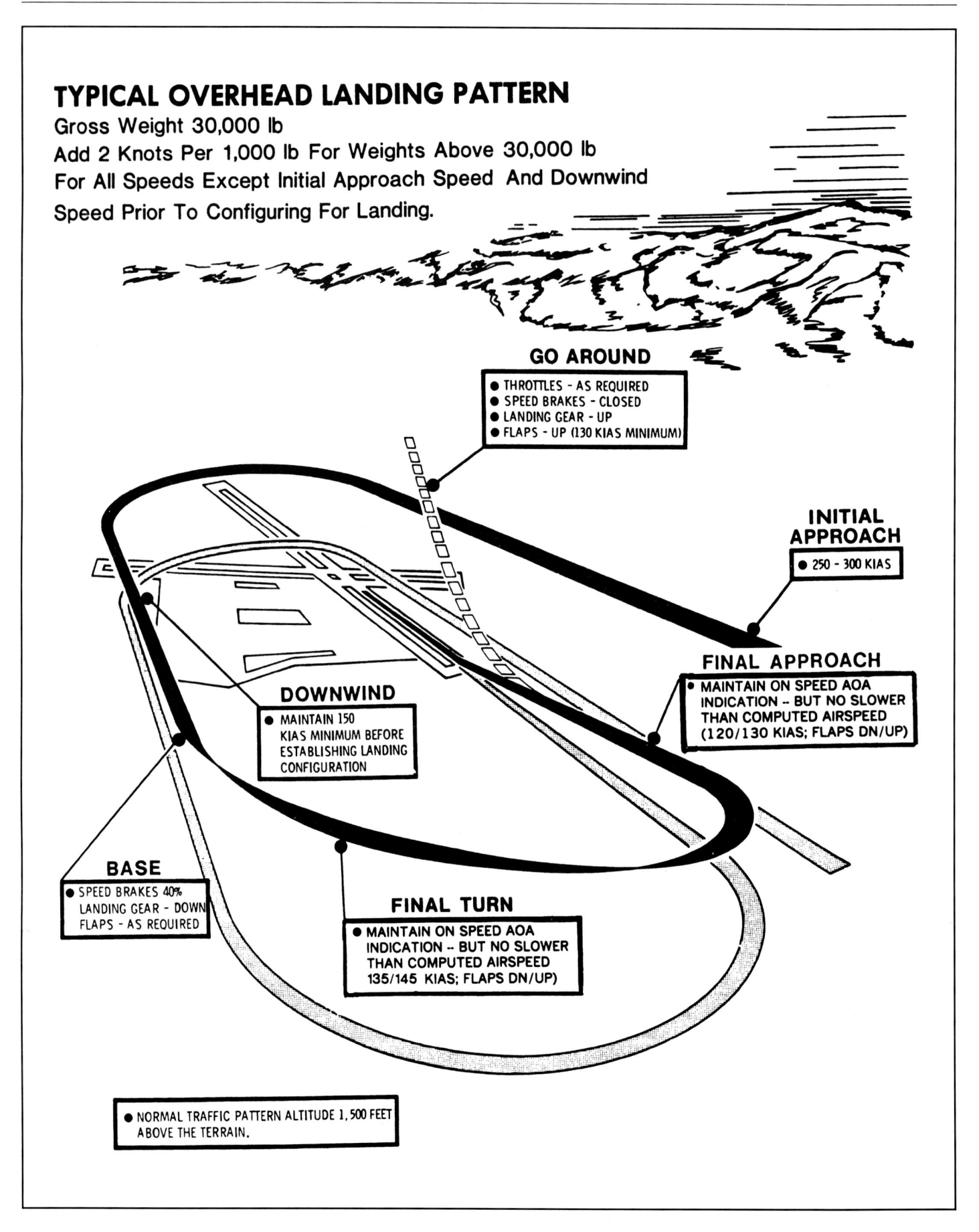

CHAPTER 3: A-10 DESCRIPTION

TYPICAL OVERHEAD LANDING PATTERN
Gross Weight 30,000 lb
Add 2 Knots Per 1,000 lb For Weights Above 30,000 lb
For All Speeds Except Initial Approach Speed And Downwind
Speed Prior To Configuring For Landing.

GO AROUND
- THROTTLES - AS REQUIRED
- SPEED BRAKES - CLOSED
- LANDING GEAR - UP
- FLAPS - UP (130 KIAS MINIMUM)

INITIAL APPROACH
- 250 - 300 KIAS

FINAL APPROACH
- MAINTAIN ON SPEED AOA INDICATION -- BUT NO SLOWER THAN COMPUTED AIRSPEED (120/130 KIAS; FLAPS DN/UP)

DOWNWIND
- MAINTAIN 150 KIAS MINIMUM BEFORE ESTABLISHING LANDING CONFIGURATION

BASE
- SPEED BRAKES 40%
- LANDING GEAR - DOWN
- FLAPS - AS REQUIRED

FINAL TURN
- MAINTAIN ON SPEED AOA INDICATION -- BUT NO SLOWER THAN COMPUTED AIRSPEED 135/145 KIAS; FLAPS DN/UP)

- NORMAL TRAFFIC PATTERN ALTITUDE 1,500 FEET ABOVE THE TERRAIN.

CHAPTER THREE

A-10 Description

THE AIRCRAFT

The A-10 is a single-seat close air support aircraft. The aircraft is a low wing, twin rudder low tail configuration powered by two high bypass turbo fan engines installed in nacelles mounted on pylons extending from the aft fuselage. Twin vertical stabilizers are mounted on the outboard tips of the horizontal tail. The wing tips are drooped to provide better lift at low speeds, and eliminate tip lift losses. The twin tails provide better low speed directional control, as well as serving to mask the IR heat signature of the engines.

The A-10 lacks many of the compound curves that make modern airplanes such as the F-15 and F-16 look so sleek, and as a result has a big advantage over these sleek jets. 98% of A-10 parts are interchangeable from airplane to airplane. Contrasted with that, are the modern fighters which have individually fitted stress skin panels. Because the skin panels on the A-10 are not stressed, they can be repaired or replaced easily in the field to keep the airplane flying and fighting. The interchangeability of landing gears, ailerons, rudders, elevators, control actuators, and engines account for the A-10's effectiveness. The tricycle forward retracting landing gear is equipped with an anti-skid system and a steerable nose wheel.

A titanium armor "bathtub" installation surrounds the cockpit. The armored cockpit is capable of repulsing direct hits from 23mm and 57mm shells. The bathtub makes up 47% of the total of 2,900 pounds of armor protection for the A-10's systems. An additional 37% is allocated for protection of the fuel system.

The primary flight controls are equipped with artificial feel devices to simulate aerodynamic feel. The elevator and aileron controls split into redundant separate systems before leaving the armor protection. The controls are powered by two independent hydraulic systems, either of which has the capability of controlling the airplane. If both hydraulic systems fail, the airplane can be flown using a manual reversion system. The ailerons consist of an upper and lower panel that become speed brakes when opened. The windshield front panel is resistant to small arms fire and birds. The ejection seat provides a zero/zero capability (zero velocity and zero altitude) with wings level either with the canopy removed or through the canopy. The armament system includes a high fire rate 30mm seven-barrel gun with ammunition stored in a drum. A variety of stores can be carried on 11 pylons, 4 on each wing and 3 on the fuselage.

The A-10 is designed to take battle damage and return home. The wings and horizontal tail surfaces are protected by triple redundancy, with three spars in each. The entire aircraft is stressed for 7.3 G's positive, clean, or 5.0 G's fully loaded, and is capable of sustaining a 3.25 G turn at 275 knots. The big straight wings give it a very tight turn capability allowing it to stay within sight of the target while avoiding direct overflight of the target and its air defenses. Because of its design the A-10 could lose one engine, half the tail, two-thirds of a wing, and chunks of the fuselage, and still keep flying.

CHAPTER 3: A-10 DESCRIPTION

AIRCRAFT DIMENSIONS

The overall dimensions of the aircraft under normal conditions of gross weight, tire and strut inflation are:

Overall length	53 ft 4 in
Wing span	57 ft 6 in
Horizontal tail span	18 ft 10 in
Height to top of fin	14 ft 8 in
Wheel base	17 ft 9 in
Wheel tread	17 ft 3 in

AIRCRAFT GROSS WEIGHT

The aircraft operating weight is approximately 28,000 pounds. This weight includes pilot, gun (full of ammunition), 11 empty pylons, oil, windshield wash, and unusable fuel. The fully loaded maximum gross weight is 47,000 pounds.

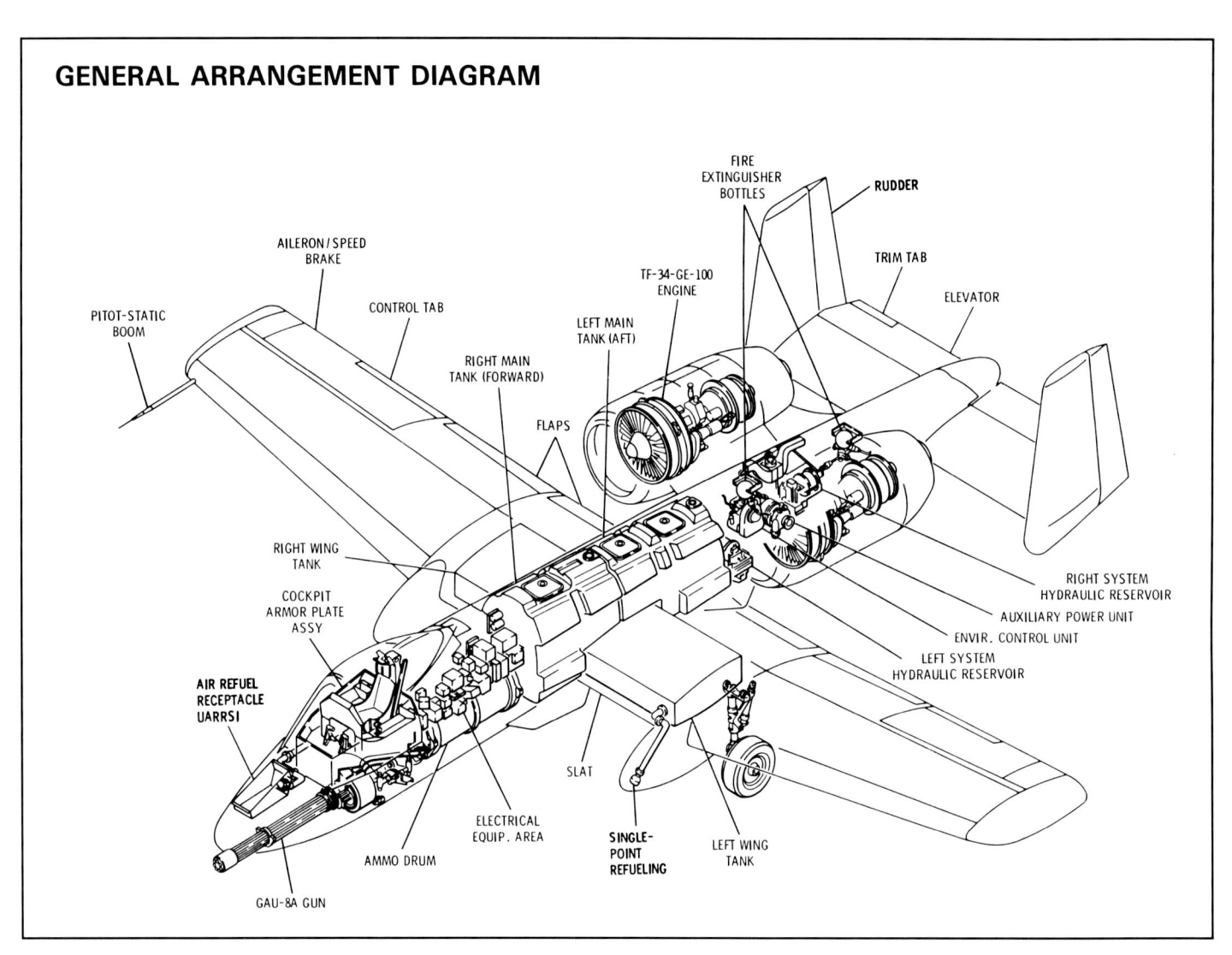

GENERAL ARRANGEMENT DIAGRAM

ENGINES

ENGINES

The aircraft is powered by two General Electric TF-34-GE100/100A engines. Sea level, standard day, static thrust for an installed engine is approximately 8,900 pounds at maximum thrust The engine incorporates a single stage bypass fan and a 14-stage axial flow compressor. Bypass air produces over 85% of engine thrust. Therefore, engine fan speed (N_1) is the best indication of thrust. Variable inlet guide vanes automatically modulate throughout the engine operating range. An accessory gearbox for each engine drives a hydraulic pump, fuel pump and fuel control, oil pump, and an electric generator. An air bleed for aircraft systems is provided. Engine acceleration time from IDLE to MAX thrust is approximately 10 seconds at sea level.

The TF-34-100 engines were pod mounted on the fuselage away from each other to enhance survivability. If one engine is hit and disintegrates, or explodes, the chances are that it will not badly damage the other engine. Also, mounting the engines high on the fuselage reduces their vulnerability to foreign object damage, caused by debris being sucked into the engines while on the ground. Mounting the engines away from the fuselage keeps the fuselage structure simple and strong, and keeps the engines away from volatile fuel bladders. Pod mounting the engines attached to the fuselage also allows space for more ordnance pylons on the underside of the wings.

AUXILIARY POWER UNIT

The APU supplies air for engine starting, drives a generator for aircraft electrical power, and can drive a hydraulic pump to pressurize the aircraft hydraulic system for ground maintenance functions. The unit is located in the aft fuselage between the two engines and has safety devices that shut down the APU if its operating limitations are exceeded.

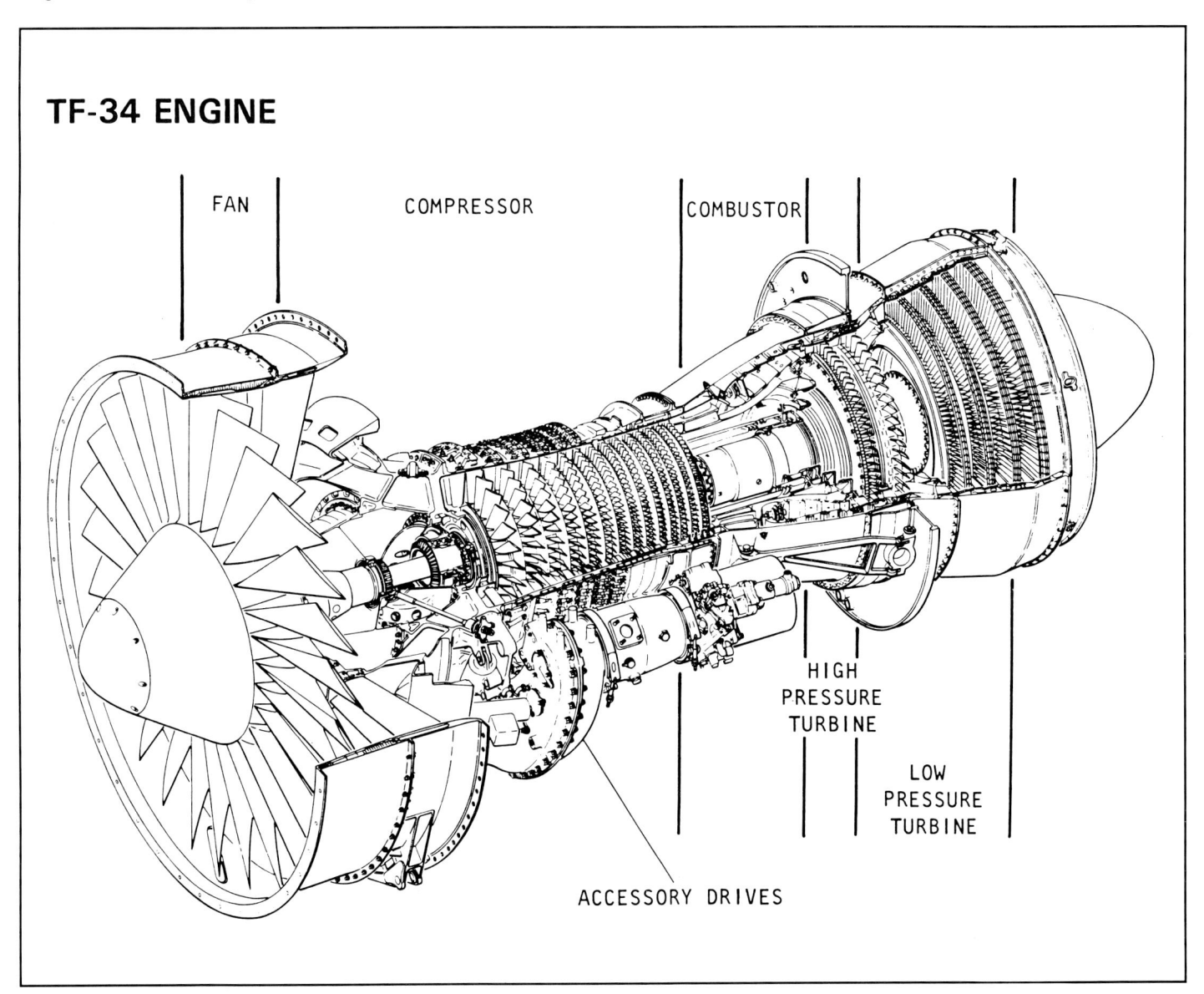

TF-34 ENGINE

CHAPTER 3: A-10 DESCRIPTION

AIRCRAFT FUEL SYSTEM

The aircraft fuel supply system consists of two internal wing tanks (left and right wing), and two tandem-mounted fuselage tanks (left main-aft and right main-forward). Up to three external (pylon) tanks may be carried; one tank under each wing and one on the fuselage centerline. The fuel supply system operates as two independent subsystems, with the left wing and left main tank feeding the left engine and the APU, and the right wing and right main tank feeding the right engine. The two subsystems can be interconnected by opening crossfeed valves (controlled by a single switch in the cockpit) to allow pressurized fuel flow to both engines and the APU from either subsystem. In addition, the two main tanks can be interconnected by opening a tank gate valve. The main tank sumps are self-sealing bladder cells. Each self-sealing sump contains approximately 900 pounds of fuel. The upper portion of the cells are tear-resistant bladders. The wing tanks are integral within the wing structure and do not have bladder cells. Foam is used in all tanks to prevent fuel tank explosion. Fuel line pressure is provided by boost pumps located in each main tank and wing tank. A boost pump, located in the left main tank is used during engine and APU starts if the left main boost pump is inoperative. For negative G flight, collector tanks supply the engine with sufficient fuel for 10 seconds operation at MAX power. The wing tank boost pumps operate at a higher pressure and override the main tank boost pumps to automatically empty the wing tanks first.

The main fuel feed lines to each engine, and to the APU, contain shutoff valves that are controlled by the fire handles. These shutoff valves allow for isolation of the fuel feed system outside the tanks. Fuel tank sump drains are provided for each tank. Drain valves can be opened externally. Fuel cavity drains are provided in each main tank, and protrude through the aircraft skin to give an indication of fuel cell leaks.

600-U.S. gallon external fuel tanks for ferry operations (the same tank designed for the F-111) may be carried on the centerline (number 6) pylon. Two more of these tanks can be carried, one on station 4 and one on station 8. Fuel in the external tanks is transferred to the main or wing tanks by pneumatic pressure from the bleed air system.

A single-point ground refueling receptacle, located in the leading edge of the left landing gear pod, permits refueling of all internal and external tanks. A control panel, adjacent to the refueling receptacle, provides a means of ground checking the refueling valve shutoff. The panel also permits selective fueling of any internal or external tank. When the tanks are full the refueling valves are closed by a float valve in each tank.

AIR REFUELING SYSTEM

The aircraft can be re fueled inflight from a boom equipped tanker. The aircraft is equipped with a UARRSI (Universal Air Refueling Receiver Slipway Installation), located on the top of the fuselage forward of the cockpit. By positioning a lever

As seen from the refueling position on the KC-10, the A-10s inflight refueling receptacle is located on the nose infront of the windshield. (USAF)

on the fuel system control panel, a flush (slipway) door, powered by the right hydraulic system, folds down into the fuselage to expose the air refueling receptacle and to provide a slipway to guide the tanker boom nozzle. When the boom nozzle is inserted in the receptacle, the nozzle latch rollers are actuated to the locked position, and fuel transfer commences. Fuel transfer through the receptacle is distributed to the main and wing tanks, and to the external tanks. Fill disable switches, located on the fuel system control panel, allow the pilot to chose specific internal tanks for fueling. As each tank is filled, float-operated fuel shutoff valves within each tank will close, preventing overfill. When refueling is completed, the disconnect of the boom nozzle will normally be accomplished by a signal from the tanker or by the receiver pilot depressing the air refuel disconnect/reset button on the control stick grip. An automatic disconnect will occur when either excessive fuel pressure occurs in the receiver fuel manifold or the tanker boom limits are exceeded. If the right hydraulic system fails, the spring-loaded slipway door will open when the air refuel control is set to OPEN.

SERVICING DIAGRAM

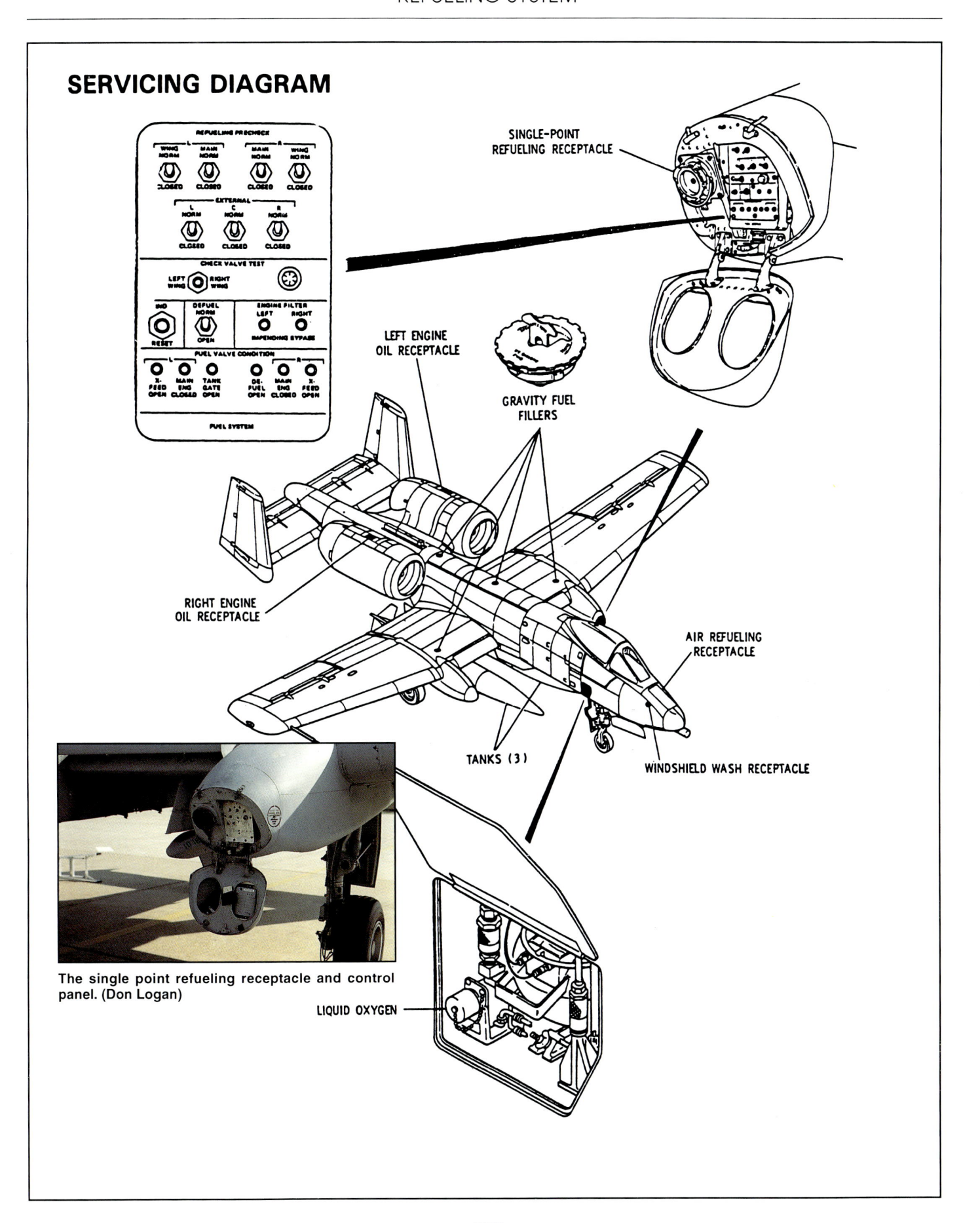

The single point refueling receptacle and control panel. (Don Logan)

CHAPTER 3: A-10 DESCRIPTION

ELECTRICAL POWER SYSTEM
The electrical power system provides DC and AC power. The battery produces DC to power essential equipment which provides the aircraft with a limited instrument flight capability. The instrument inverter changes DC from the battery to AC to power essential equipment. DC produced by the battery is adequate to start the APU. When running, the APU generator produces sufficient AC and DC to power all electrical busses indefinitely, provided electrical load is minimized. With engines running, two generators take over production of AC and DC and power all busses. External power can also be used to power all busses.

HYDRAULIC POWER SUPPLY SYSTEM
The hydraulic power supply system consists of two fully independent hydraulic systems, designated left and right. Both systems are pressurized by identical engine driven pumps. A small accumulator in each system stabilizes system pressure. In addition to the two system hydraulic pumps, an APU hydraulic pump can be used on the ground to provide hydraulic power to either hydraulic system, but not both simultaneously.

The left hydraulic system powers:
Flight control – Left rudder, left elevator, left and right aileron, flaps
Landing gear – Landing gear extend and retract, wheel brakes, anti-skid, and nose wheel steering
Armament – One half of gun drive

The right hydraulic system powers:
Flight control – Right rudder, right elevator, left and right aileron, speed brakes, slats
Emergency – Auxiliary landing gear extend systems, emergency wheel braking and associated accumulators
Armament – One half of gun drive
Air refueling – Slipway door and receptacle lock.

The hydraulic systems are designed for combat survivability. The left and right systems are physically separated as much as possible. The landing gear, gear uplock, wheel brake, and nose wheel steering lines are isolated from the left system pressure when the gear is up and locked. The landing gear and associated systems can also be isolated from the left hydraulic system. The speed brakes can be isolated from right system. Flaps can be totally isolated from the left hydraulic system.

LANDING GEAR SYSTEM
The landing gear system is a tricycle configuration with the main gear retracting into pods below the wing and the nose gear retracting into the fuselage. The nose gear is offset to the right of the aircraft centerline to accommodate the centerline location of the 30mm gun. All three landing gear struts, retract forward to aid free-fall auxiliary extension. Landing gear extension and retraction is controlled by the landing gear handle and powered by the left hydraulic system. In the gear-retracted position, the system is depressurized and isolated. In the normal gear down position, the system is pressurized.

Main Landing Gear
The shock struts provide a rough field taxi capability. The landing gear retracting cylinder is also the drag brace. A spring-powered mechanical downlock automatically engages both for powered and free-fall gear extensions. Switches provide cockpit indication of downlock.

For gear retraction, hydraulic pressure unlocks the downlock and then extends the retracting cylinder piston to push (rotate) the gear forward and up. As the gear approaches the upstop, an uplock is engaged. Also, gear up pressure automatically applies brake pressure to stop wheel rotation before the wheels retract into the gear pods.

For gear extension, hydraulic pressure disengages the uplock hooks and simultaneously retracts the cylinder piston to pull down the gear. Extend pressure is maintained with the gear handle in DOWN. When retracted, a spring-loaded snubber contacts the tire to prevent air drag rotation of the wheels.

Nose Landing Gear
The nose landing gear operates similar to the main gear. As the strut extends when weight comes off the tire, a cam centers the nose wheel. Two doors seal off the fuselage compartment after gear retraction.

PRIMARY FLIGHT CONTROL SYSTEM
Pilot commands are transmitted via pushrods from the stick to the aft area of the armored cockpit, through a set of control disconnectors, and then by redundant cables to the elevators and ailerons, and by a single cable to the rudders. Loss of one hydraulic system does not affect pitch and roll response but does cause moderate increase in pedal force required for yaw inputs. Jams in the pitch or roll control systems, aft of the disconnect units may be isolated to free the stick for control of the unjammed portions. Yaw control is provided by two rudders, which are individually driven by independent hydraulic actuators. The pitch and roll axes have redundant control circuits for trim controls, while yaw trim is through the yaw Stability Augmentation System (SAS). The dual channel SAS provides rate damping in both the pitch and yaw axes as well as automatic turn coordination.

MANUAL REVERSION FLIGHT CONTROL SYSTEM
The Manual Reversion Flight Control System, (MRFCS), is an emergency system for use when dual hydraulic failure is impending or has occurred. The mode is adequate for executing moderate maneuvers and for safe return to base and landing. Emergency transitions to manual reversion are automatic and instantaneous in pitch and yaw, with stick and pedal commands transmitted directly to the elevator and rudder surfaces through the actuators, which are in the hydraulic bypass mode. Transitions in roll must be pilot initiated.

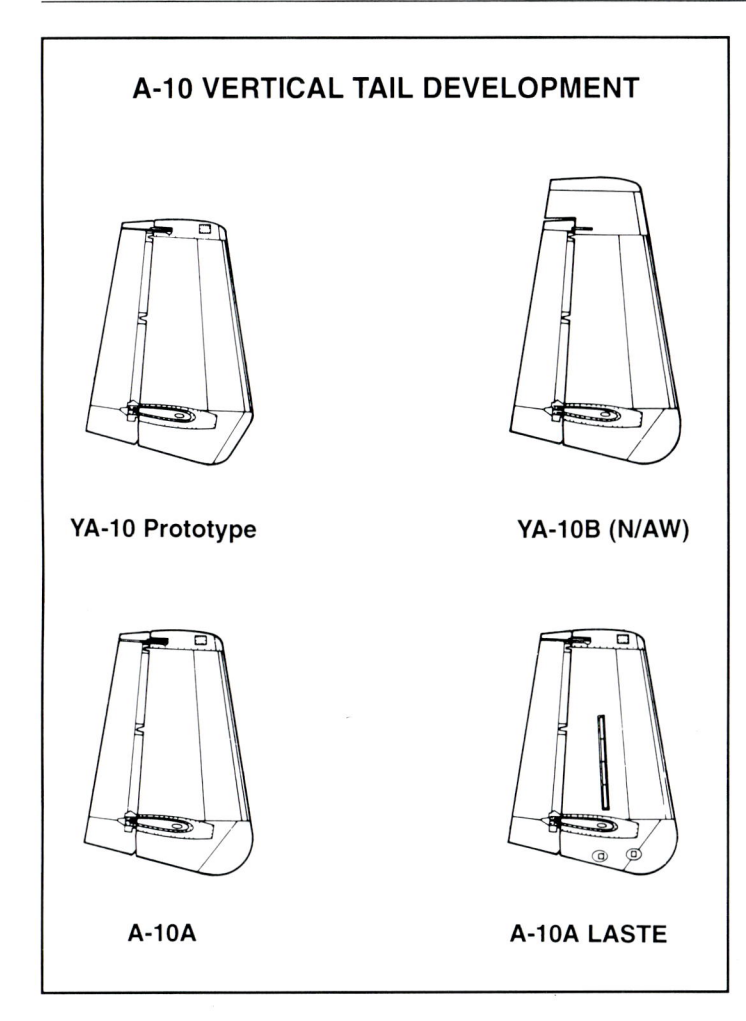

POWER SYSTEMS/LANDING GEAR/FLIGHT CONTROL SYSTEM

A-10 VERTICAL TAIL DEVELOPMENT

YA-10 Prototype

YA-10B (N/AW)

A-10A

A-10A LASTE

The ailerons open to act as speed brakes. (Don Logan)

SECONDARY FLIGHT CONTROL SYSTEM

Speed Brake System
The speed brake surfaces and actuators are integrated in the ailerons. The upper and lower surfaces of both ailerons open to act as speed brakes. The speed brakes fully open or close in approximately 3 seconds. The speed brakes are limited to 80% open position in flight.

Flap System
The aircraft is equipped with four wing trailing edge flaps. Flap positions are 0 (flaps up-UP), 7 (maneuvering flaps - MVR), and 20 (flaps down-DN). The flaps are individually supported and each flap is positioned by one hydraulic actuator. The flaps are powered by the left hydraulic system. A cockpit control lever controls the position of the flaps. When extended, flaps hold position in the event of loss of flap system electrical and/or hydraulic power until commanded up by the flap emergency retract switch. On loss of the left hydraulic system, the flaps will be inoperative. When fully extended, aerodynamic forces will cause unpowered flaps to retract to less than 15 and maneuvering flaps to retract to 0 if the emergency flap switch is activated. In full up or full down, hydraulic pressure is retained in the selected position to eliminate flap creeping. The left outboard flap will cycle about the 7 position, and the other flap panels may assume varying positions. It may be necessary to recycle the flap lever to get all panels back to the 7 position.

Slat System
The slat system consists of movable two-position slat panels which are mounted on the inboard leading edge section of each wing. Slats are hydraulic powered. The slats function automatically to improve high AOA air flow to the engines. The ESPS detects conditions that will lead to engine stall. Stall is determined in the ESPS system as a function of AOA and Mach. The AOA is measured by a lift transducer mounted on the lower side of the left wing leading edge. Mach is measured internally in the ESPS through the pitot static system. At a predetermined AOA and Mach, the slats extend.

CHAPTER 3: A-10 DESCRIPTION

EJECTION SEAT

The first production A-10s (Number 1 through 101) had the ESCAPAC ejection seat. Starting with aircraft #102 (77-0177) the A-10s received the McDonnell-Douglas ACES II ejection seat. The early aircraft were retrofitted with ACES II seats.

The ACES II ejection seat is a fully automatic catapult rocket system. Three ejection modes are automatically selected. Mode 1 is a low speed mode during which the parachute is deployed almost immediately after the seat departs the aircraft. Mode 2 is a high speed mode during which a drogue chute is first deployed to slow the seat, followed by the deployment of the parachute. Mode 3 is a high altitude mode in which the sequence of events is the same as Mode 2, except that man-seat separation and deployment of the parachute is delayed until a safe altitude is reached. Controls are provided to adjust seat height and lock shoulder harness.

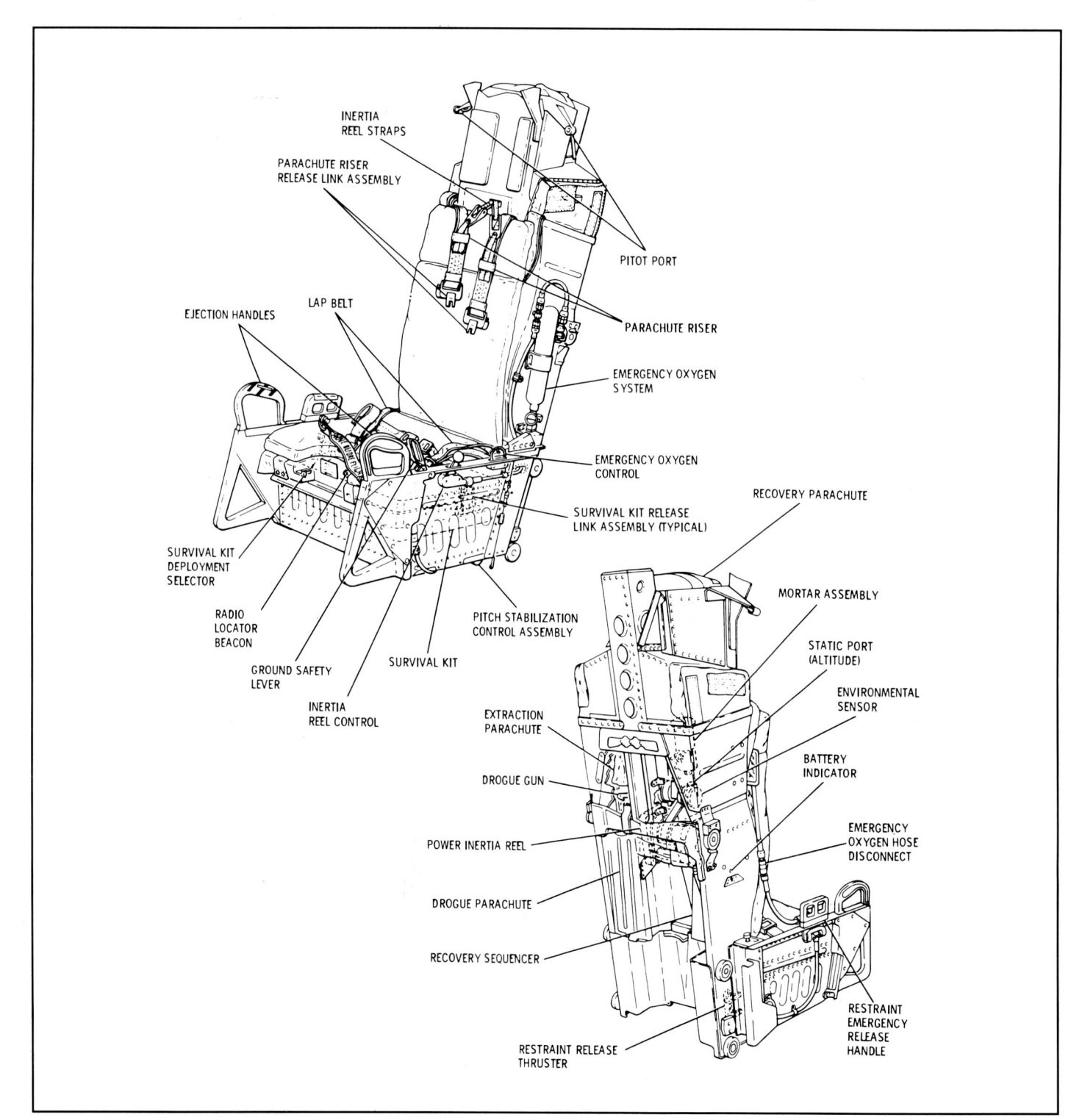

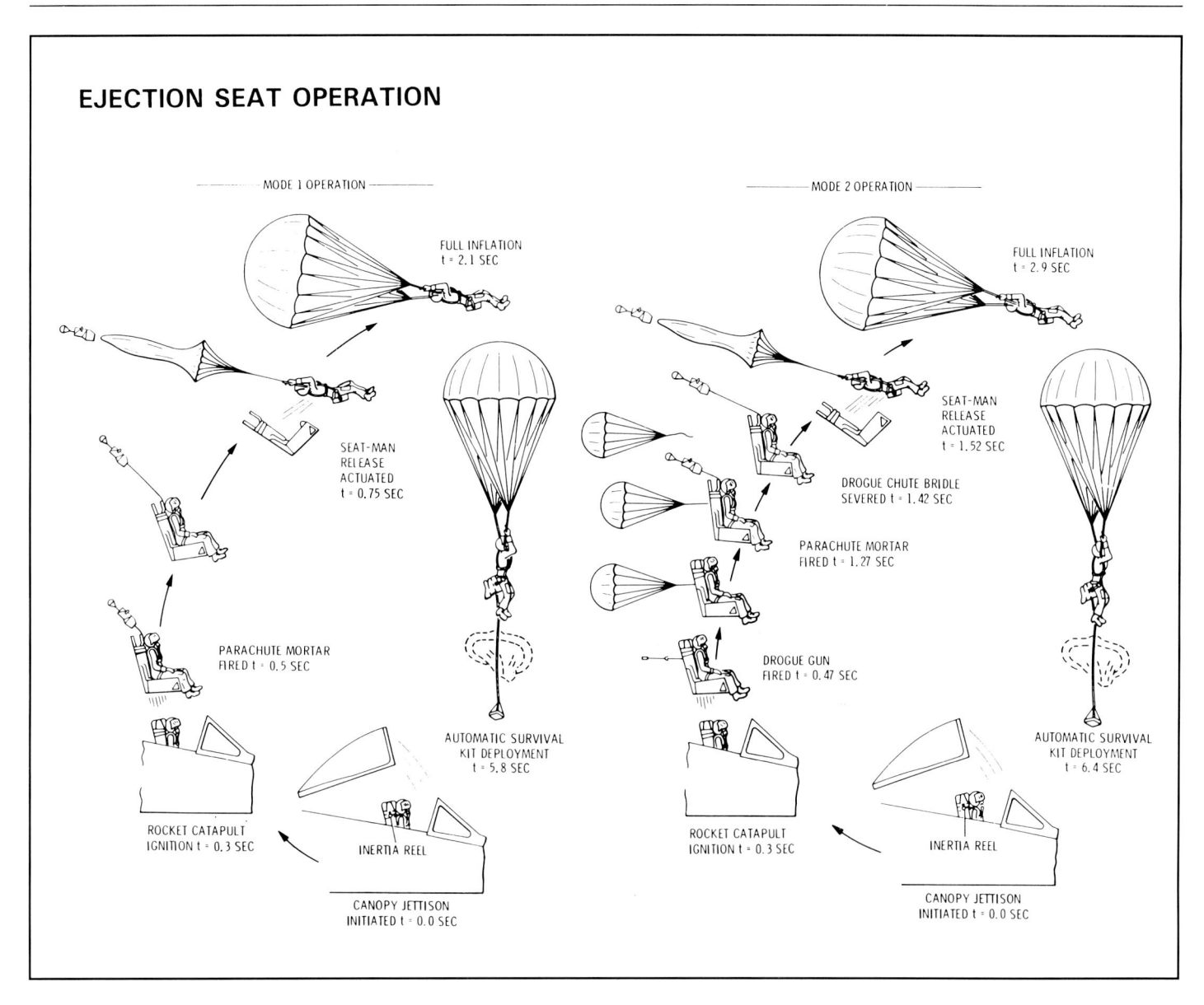

EJECTION SEAT/ENVIRONMENTAL CONTROL SYSTEM/COMMUNICATIONS

EJECTION SEAT OPERATION

MODE 1 OPERATION
- FULL INFLATION t = 2.1 SEC
- SEAT-MAN RELEASE ACTUATED t = 0.75 SEC
- PARACHUTE MORTAR FIRED t = 0.5 SEC
- AUTOMATIC SURVIVAL KIT DEPLOYMENT t = 5.8 SEC
- ROCKET CATAPULT IGNITION t = 0.3 SEC
- INERTIA REEL
- CANOPY JETTISON INITIATED t = 0.0 SEC

MODE 2 OPERATION
- FULL INFLATION t = 2.9 SEC
- SEAT-MAN RELEASE ACTUATED t = 1.52 SEC
- DROGUE CHUTE BRIDLE SEVERED t = 1.42 SEC
- PARACHUTE MORTAR FIRED t = 1.27 SEC
- DROGUE GUN FIRED t = 0.47 SEC
- AUTOMATIC SURVIVAL KIT DEPLOYMENT t = 6.4 SEC
- ROCKET CATAPULT IGNITION t = 0.3 SEC
- INERTIA REEL
- CANOPY JETTISON INITIATED t = 0.0 SEC

ENVIRONMENTAL CONTROL SYSTEM

The environmental control system supplies temperature controlled air for cockpit air conditioning and pressurization. The system also provides service air for windshield and canopy defogging, windshield rain removal, canopy seal, anti-G suit pressurization, and external tank pressurization. The environmental control system receives bleed air from the engines, the APU, or an external source. The airflow rate to the cockpit is controlled by means of the flow level control on the environment control panel. The temperature controller automatically maintains the selected mixed airflow temperature level. If the environment system becomes inoperative, the cockpit can be ventilated by ram air.

Cockpit pressurization is ensured by use of a canopy seal system and a cockpit air pressure regulator. Cockpit pressurization is automatically initiated at 10,000 feet and is controlled by the cockpit air pressure regulator. Regulator discharge air assists in cooling equipment in the electronic and avionics compartments. If the regulator fails, a cockpit air pressure safety valve automatically opens.

COMMUNICATION AND NAVIGATION EQUIPMENT

Communication Equipment

Radios
The A-10 is equipped with radios for communications on the VHF/FM Band (30 to 76 MHz), VHF/AM Band (116.00 to 151.975 MHz) and UHF Band (225.000 to 399.975 MHz).

Intercom
The AIC-18 Intercommunications system gives the pilot the capability of monitoring audio signals, including warning tones. During ground operations the intercom is used for voice communication with the ground crew.

CHAPTER 3: A-10 DESCRIPTION

ANTENNA LOCATIONS/IFF CODING

- RADAR WARNING
- UHF/TACAN
- IFF
- RADAR WARNING
- C/D BAND RADAR WARNING OR L-BAND RADAR WARNING
- RADAR WARNING
- RADAR WARNING
- IFF MODE 2 CODE ACCESS
- IFF
- UHF/TACAN
- VHF/AM
- VHF/FM
- MARKER BEACON
- UHF/ADF
- RADAR WARNING
- RADAR WARNING
- UHF/TACAN
- VHF/FM/HOMING
- LOCALIZER/GLIDE SLOPE
- CHAFF/FLARE PROGRAMMER CONTROL

NAVIGATION/RADAR WARNING/DEFENSIVE ORDNANCE

Navigation Equipment

Transponder
The AN/APX-101 IFF Transponder provides automatic radar identification to suitable equipped challenging aircraft, surface ships, and ground facilities within range.

TACAN
The AN/ARN-118(V) TACAN provides navigational information of range and bearing to a surface TACAN station or another aircraft equipped with a similar TACAN system.

RADAR WARNING EQUIPMENT
Initially one of four radar warning systems was installed in the A-10. Aircraft prior to 75-0299 had the basic AN/ALR-46(V). Aircraft from 75-0299 to 76-0554 had an AN/ALR-46A (redesignated AN/ALR-46(V)-3). Aircraft from 77—177 to 77-0276 had an AN/ALR-64 (redesignated AN/ALR-46(V)-9). Aircraft 78-0582 and up had an AN/ALR-69 installed.

Aircraft up to 76-0554 were later modified installing the AN/ALR-46(V)-9. With this mod, only two types of radar warning equipment is now installed in the A-10. Aircraft before 78-0582 have the AN/ALR-46(V)-9, and aircraft 78-0582 and newer have the AN/ALR-69(V).

Both the radar warning systems provide the capability to detect missile activity and missile launch conditions using three data files; land, sea, and training. The system displays the missile system data using lights on the control indicator unit and the quadrant in which a missile guidance tracking radar is operating on the azimuth indicator.

DEFENSIVE ORDNANCE
The primary defensive armament of the A-10 is two AIM-9L/M Sidewinders. The A-10 is capable of carrying all types of AIM-9 missiles. The AIM-9s are mounted on LAU-105 launcher rails, two rail are mounted on a dual rail adaptor (DRA). The launcher is normally mounted on the left outboard wing station (number one, unless there is a wiring problem on that particular aircraft, in which case it is mounted on the opposing station (number 11).

For combat, an ECM pods are normally mounted on the wing station opposite the AIM-9s (usually number 11). During the time frame of Desert Storm, A-10 deployed from continental U.S. bases normally carried an ALQ-119(V)-15 pods covering all bands, while Shallow ALQ-131(V) pods were carried on overseas-based aircraft. The ALQ-184(V)-1 and Deep ALQ-131 are also authorized for use. The A-10 has the capability of carrying the AN/ALQ-119(V)-10, -12, -15, and -17. AN/ALQ-131(V)-1 through -13 and 15, AN/ALQ-184(V)-2, and QRC 80-01(V)-3 can also be carried.

A-10s carry ALE-40(V) chaff and flare countermeasures dispensers under their wingtips and at the back of the main landing gear pods. The dispensers can carry RR-170 A/AL chaff cartridges and M-206 Flare Cartridges.

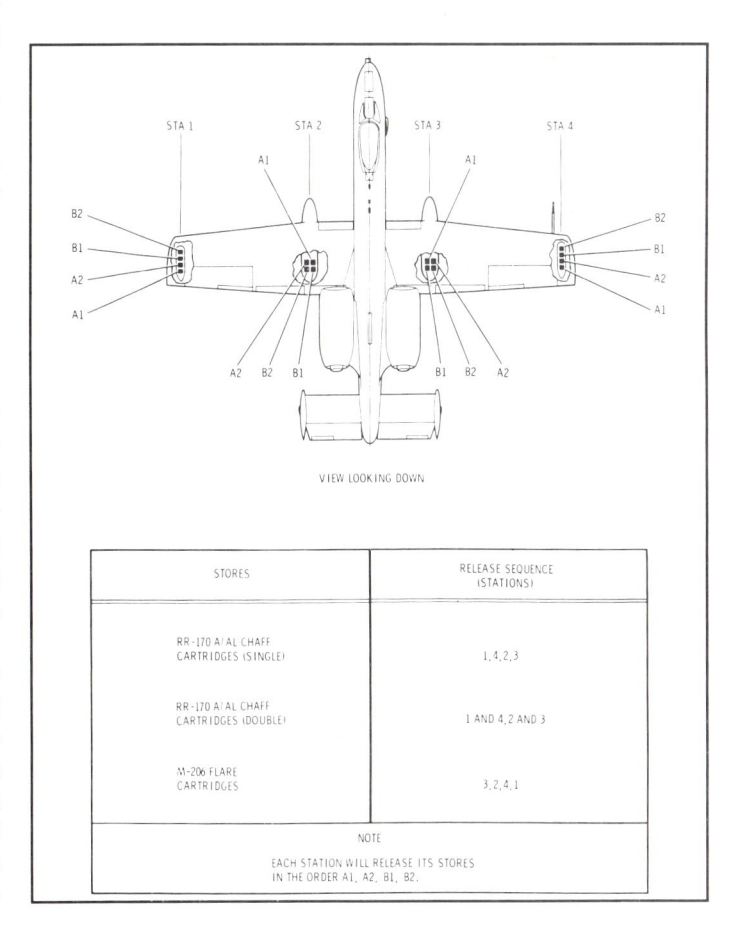

A chaff/flare dispenser is located beneath each wing tip. (Don Logan)

STORES	RELEASE SEQUENCE (STATIONS)
RR-170 A/AL CHAFF CARTRIDGES (SINGLE)	1, 4, 2, 3
RR-170 A/AL CHAFF CARTRIDGES (DOUBLE)	1 AND 4, 2 AND 3
M-206 FLARE CARTRIDGES	3, 2, 4, 1
NOTE: EACH STATION WILL RELEASE ITS STORES IN THE ORDER A1, A2, B1, B2.	

211

CHAPTER 3: A-10 DESCRIPTION

AN/ALQ-119(V) ECM POD

- A4 — AFT ANTENNA MODULE
- A3 — MID/HIGH BAND MODULE
- A2 — LOW BAND MODULE
- A1 — FORWARD ANTENNA MODULE

(V)-15 ALL BAND

CHARACTERISTICS

	(V)-15
WEIGHT	580 LB
LENGTH	12 FT 11 IN.
WIDTH	12 IN.
HEIGHT	21 IN.
SUSPENSION LUGS	30 IN.

- ANTENNA/SERVICE MODULE
- LOW BAND MODULE (HEAT EXCHANGER)
- MID/HIGH BAND MODULE (HEAT EXCHANGER)
- FORWARD ANTENNA MODULE

AN/ALQ-184(V)-1

CHARACTERISTICS

	(V)-1
HEIGHT	20 IN.
WIDTH	10 IN.
LENGTH	13 FT.
WEIGHT	625 LB.
SUSPENSION LUG SPACING	30 IN.

AN/ALQ-131(V) ECM PODS

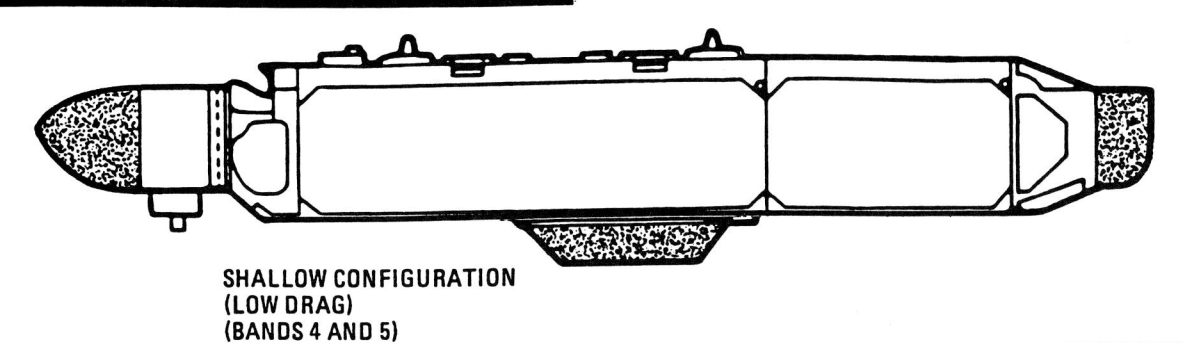

SHALLOW CONFIGURATION
(LOW DRAG)
(BANDS 4 AND 5)

DEEP CONFIGURATION
(BANDS 3, 4, AND 5)

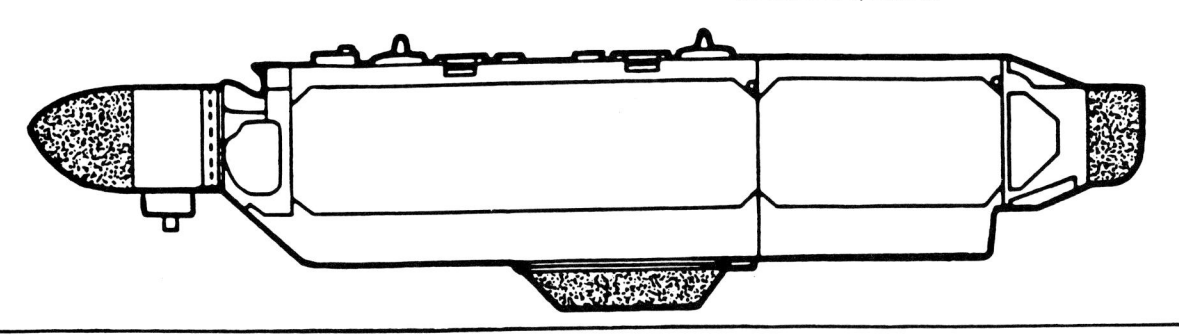

CHARACTERISTICS

SHALLOW CONFIGURATION	BLOCK I	BLOCK II
SUSPENSION LUG SPACING	30 IN.	
HEIGHT	20 IN.	
LENGTH	111 IN.	
WEIGHT		
-9, -10	600 LBS.	
-13		540 LBS.
-15		580 LBS.

DEEP CONFIGURATION	BLOCK I	BLOCK II
SUSPENSION LUG SPACING	30 IN.	
HEIGHT	24.5 IN.	
LENGTH	111 IN.	
WEIGHT		
-4, -5, -6	675 LBS.	
-12		640 LBS.
-14		680 LBS.

AN/AA-35(V)(1) PAVE PENNY LASER TARGET IDENTIFICATION SET

The PAVE PENNY is a forward looking laser seeker and tracker system. The system consists of a laser illumination detector pod and control panel. The pod cannot designate, but only receives reflected laser energy. The 32 pound detector pod attaches to a special pylon mounted on the right side of the aircraft below the cockpit. The system searches for coded laser energy reflected from a target which has been illuminated by a coded laser designator. The pod will lock on and track the reflected laser light to provide target location indicator to the A-10's avionics system. The target location indicator is then displayed on the head-up display (HUD) and/ or the attitude director indicator (ADI).

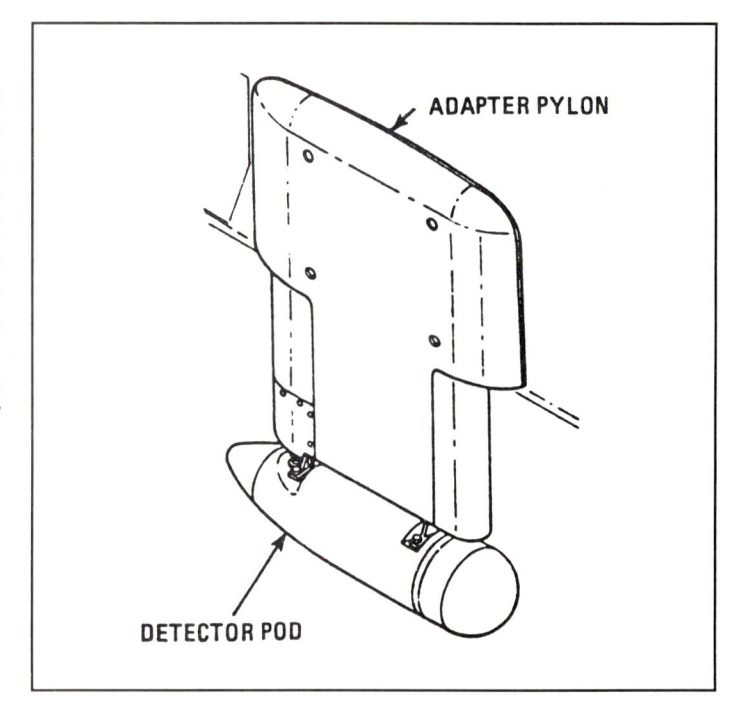

The A-10 has a capability of carrying a Pave Penny pod like this one on a pylon on the right side of the fuselage below the cockpit. (Norris Graser)

A-10 WEAPONS

The A-10 has 11 pylon stations capable of carrying weapons in addition to the GAU-8 cannon in the nose. The number 1 pylon station is outboard on the left wingtip out approximately two thirds of the distance between the main landing gear and the wing tip. The number 11 pylon station is in a symmetrical position on the right. Stations 5, 6, and 7 are on the fuselage, with stations 4 and 8 inboard of the main landing gear pods. The other stations are outboard of these pods. Stations 3, 4, 5, 7, 8, and 9 can carry triple ejector racks (TERs) on the pylon. The pylons on stations 2/10 and 5/7 can be removed in high threat areas to improve maneuverability. The centerline pylon (station 6) is normally not loaded for combat operations, and is most often used to carry a 600-U.S. gallon fuel tank for ferry operations. Two more of these auxiliary fuel tanks can be carried on stations 4 and 8.

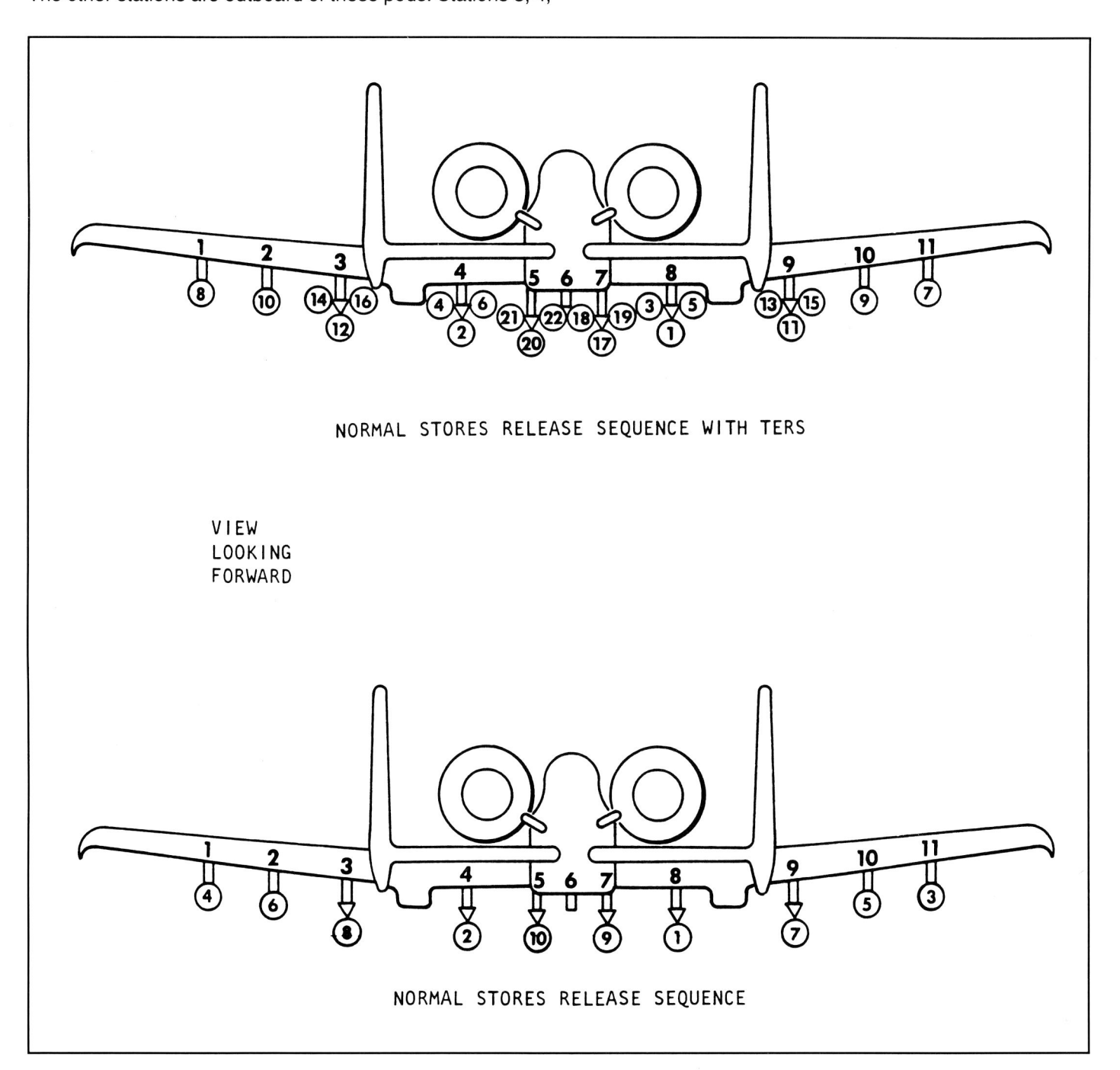

NORMAL STORES RELEASE SEQUENCE WITH TERS

VIEW LOOKING FORWARD

NORMAL STORES RELEASE SEQUENCE

CHAPTER 3: A-10 DESCRIPTION

GAU-8 Avenger Cannon

The 30mm GAU-8 cannon, designed for destroying armored vehicles is mounted on the centerline of the aircraft. The gun fires at rates of 2,000 to 4,000 rounds per minute (with an average recoil from one round of 10,000 pounds). The gun is mounted on the aircraft centerline, with the nose landing gear offset to the right. With the gun mounted on the centerline, its recoil will not impart yaw to the aircraft when fired. The GAU-8 bullet's trajectory is almost flat, making it deadly at a range of 4,000 feet, and with a well placed shot capable of knocking out a tank at 6,000 feet. Lightly armored vehicles can be destroyed at two miles. The gun has three type of projectiles (bullets); PGU-15/B Target Practice (TP) round, PGU-14/B Armor-Piercing Incendiary (API) round, and PGU-13/B High Explosive incendiary (HEI) round. The TP round is an inert projectile. The API round contains a depleted uranium penetrator, a non-discarding aluminum carrier and a nose cap. The API round consists of a fragmenting steel body, a modified M505 fuze, and an HE incendiary mix.

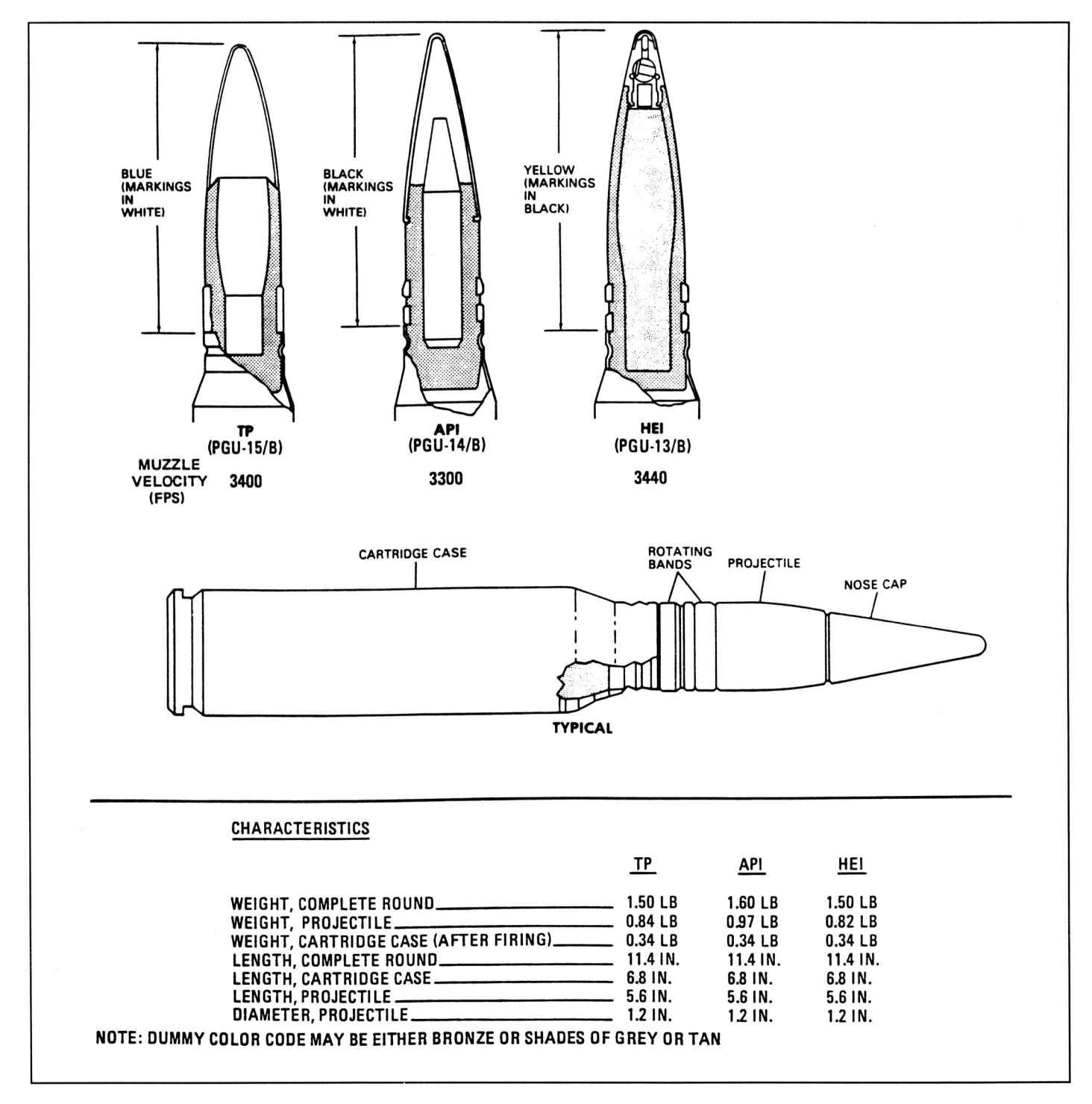

	TP (PGU-15/B)	API (PGU-14/B)	HEI (PGU-13/B)
Color	BLUE (MARKINGS IN WHITE)	BLACK (MARKINGS IN WHITE)	YELLOW (MARKINGS IN BLACK)
MUZZLE VELOCITY (FPS)	3400	3300	3440

CHARACTERISTICS

	TP	API	HEI
WEIGHT, COMPLETE ROUND	1.50 LB	1.60 LB	1.50 LB
WEIGHT, PROJECTILE	0.84 LB	0.97 LB	0.82 LB
WEIGHT, CARTRIDGE CASE (AFTER FIRING)	0.34 LB	0.34 LB	0.34 LB
LENGTH, COMPLETE ROUND	11.4 IN.	11.4 IN.	11.4 IN.
LENGTH, CARTRIDGE CASE	6.8 IN.	6.8 IN.	6.8 IN.
LENGTH, PROJECTILE	5.6 IN.	5.6 IN.	5.6 IN.
DIAMETER, PROJECTILE	1.2 IN.	1.2 IN.	1.2 IN.

NOTE: DUMMY COLOR CODE MAY BE EITHER BRONZE OR SHADES OF GREY OR TAN

A-10 WEAPONS

Missiles and Rockets

One of the A-10's primary weapons is the AGM-65 Maverick missile. During Desert Storm, A-10s launched 5,013 AGM-65 Mavericks. This was 90% of the Air Force total. Mavericks are carried only carried on stations 3 and 9, the first station outboard of the landing gear pods. For carriage and launch, Mavericks are carried on single rail LAU-117 launchers or triple-rail LAU-88s launchers. Four types of AGM-65s, the electro-optical(EO) A and B models, and imaging infra-red (IIR) D and G models, are capable of being carried and launched by the A-10. The aft sections of the A, B, and D models of the Maverick missiles carry a 125-lb conical shaped-charge warhead, in front of the rocket motor, designed for use against armor or reinforced structures. The G model AGM-65 has a larger aft section which carries a 300-lb blast warhead in front of the rocket. This warhead is designed to be used against targets such as GCI and SAM sites. The AGM-65G can only be launched from the from the single rail LAU-117. IIR Mavericks can be used at night as a poor-man's FLIR system using their infra-red sensor to display images to hunt for targets. The AA 37A-T1 Training Guided Missile (TGM-65) is carried for training.

The A-10 carries LAU-68 or LAU-131 rocket launchers, each capable of carrying 7 rockets. The LAU-68 can carry 2.75-in FFAR with MK-4 or MK-40 motors and MK-1(high explosive), MK-5 (anti-armor), M151 (fragmentation), M156 (white phosphorous), WDU-4A/A (flechette), WDU-13/A (flechette) warheads; or MK-61 and WTU-1/B practice warheads. The LAU-131 can carry 2.75 FFARs with MK-40 or MK-66 motors and MK-1, MK-5, MK-151, MK-156, MK-67 (red phosphorous), WDU-4A/A, WDU-13/A, MK-61, and WTLL-1/B warheads.

Forward firing target marking white phosphorous (WP), or "Willie Peter," 2.75-in Folding Fin Aircraft Rocket (FFAR) are used by OA-10As as part of their Forward Air Control (FAC) mission to mark targets.

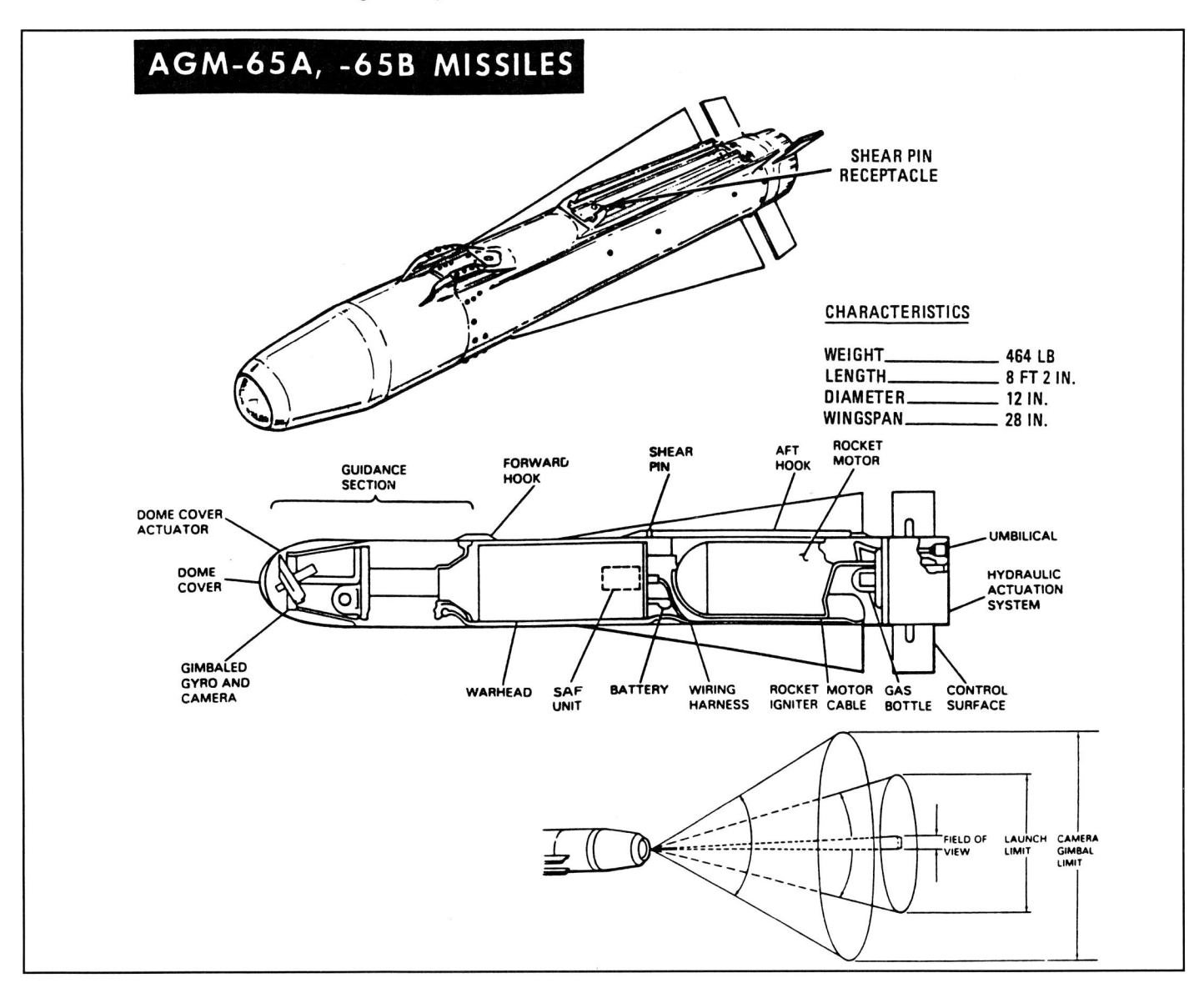

AGM-65A, -65B MISSILES

CHARACTERISTICS

WEIGHT	464 LB
LENGTH	8 FT 2 IN.
DIAMETER	12 IN.
WINGSPAN	28 IN.

CHAPTER 3: A-10 DESCRIPTION

Flares and Target Markers Flares

LUU-2 flares can be carried by the OA-10A/A-10. LUU-2 flares are used for lighting an area and burn at an average of 2 million candle power for five minutes. Target marker flares, the LUU-1/B (red), LUU-5/B (green), or LUU-6/B (maroon) are used by OA-10As and A-10s to identify or mark targets. The target markers differ from illumination flares in that they burn for 30 minutes at 1,000 candlepower. The flares/target markers are carried in a SUU-25 flare dispensers. The dispenser has four tubes with two flares in each tube. The flares are ejected out of the aft of the tubes. SUU-25s can be mounted singly on stations 2, 3, 9, and 10, and on TERs on stations 3 and 9.

LUU-2 FLARE PROFILE

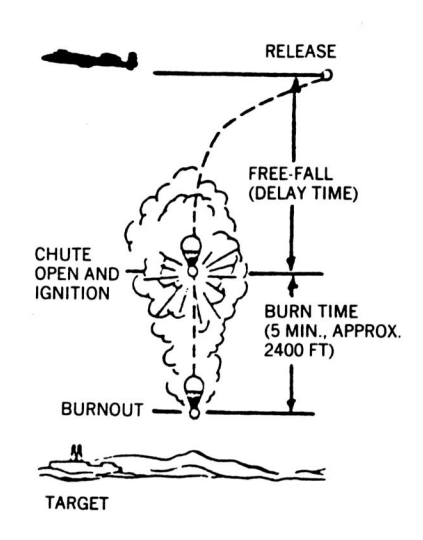

LUU-2/B, LUU-2A/B AND LUU-2B/B FLARE

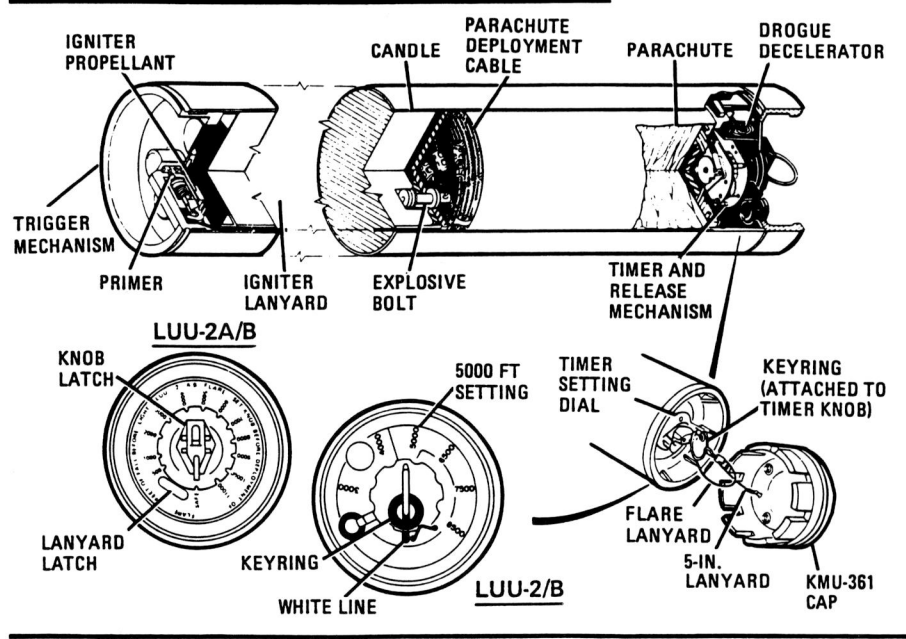

CHARACTERISTICS

WEIGHT	29 LB
LENGTH	3 FT
DIAMETER	5 IN.

FLARES AND TARGET MARKERS

LUU-1/B, 5/B, 6/B TARGET MARKER FLARES

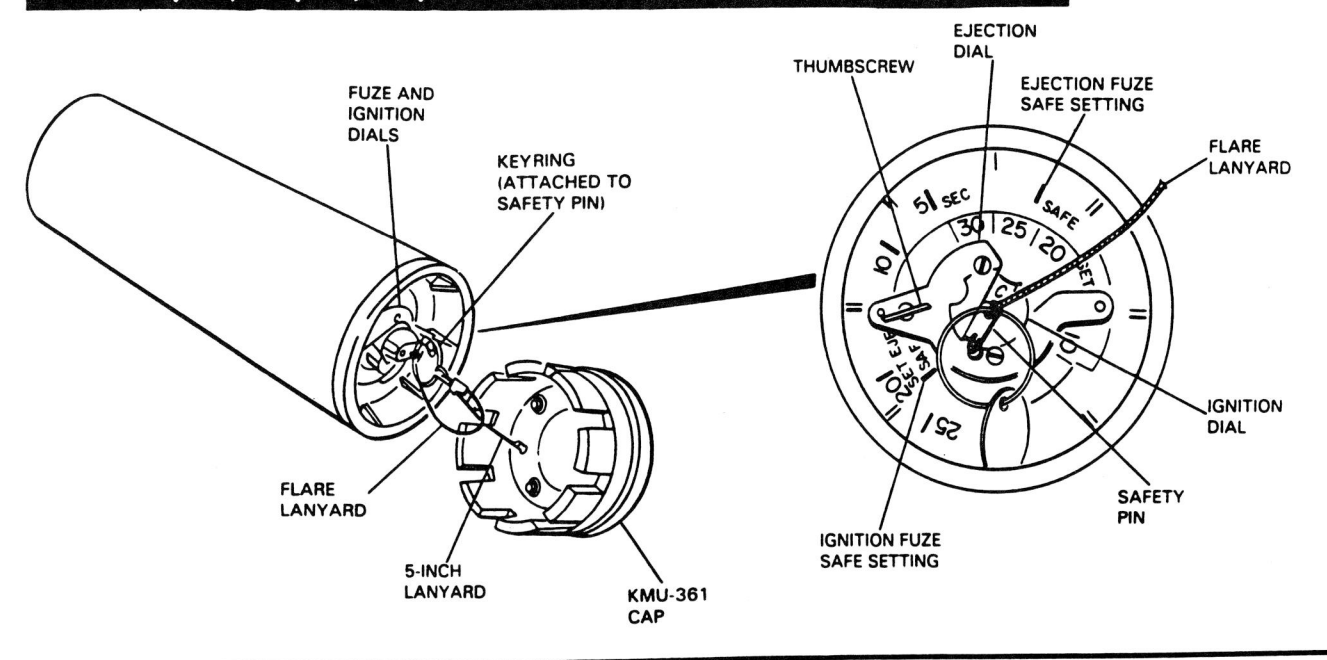

Labels: FUZE AND IGNITION DIALS; KEYRING (ATTACHED TO SAFETY PIN); FLARE LANYARD; 5-INCH LANYARD; KMU-361 CAP; THUMBSCREW; EJECTION DIAL; EJECTION FUZE SAFE SETTING; FLARE LANYARD; IGNITION DIAL; SAFETY PIN; IGNITION FUZE SAFE SETTING

CHARACTERISTICS

WEIGHT	26 LB
LENGTH	36 IN.
DIAMETER	4.87 IN.

LUU-1/B, 5/B, 6/B RELEASE PROFILE

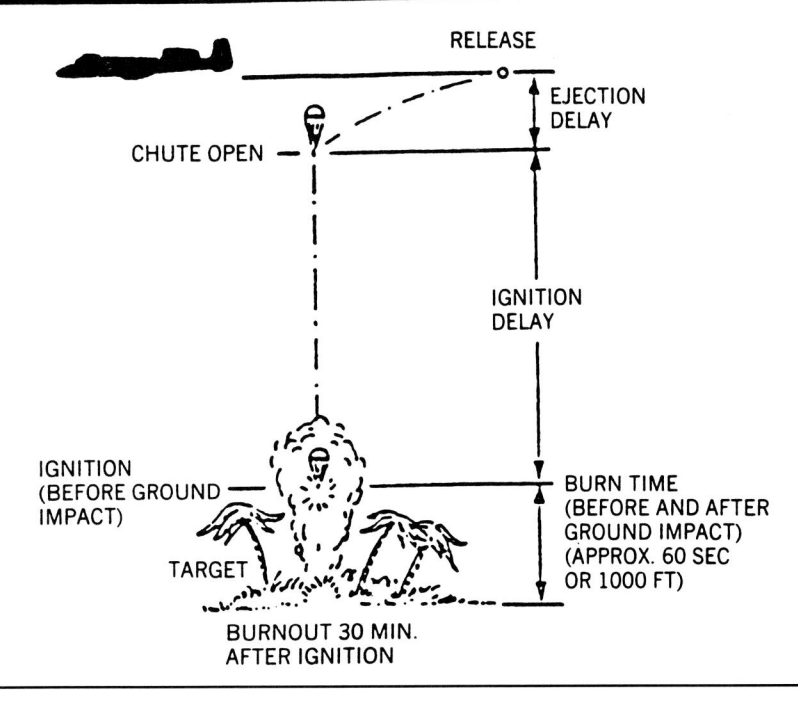

Labels: RELEASE; EJECTION DELAY; CHUTE OPEN; IGNITION DELAY; IGNITION (BEFORE GROUND IMPACT); TARGET; BURN TIME (BEFORE AND AFTER GROUND IMPACT) (APPROX. 60 SEC OR 1000 FT); BURNOUT 30 MIN. AFTER IGNITION

219

CHAPTER 3: A-10 DESCRIPTION

Gravity Weapons

Gravity bombs of less than 1,000 lb (451 kg) can be loaded on Triple Ejector Racks (TERs) on stations 3, 4, 5, 7, 8, and 9, or singly on all stations except station 6. 1,000 pound class ordnance can only be carried on stations 3,4,5,7,8, and 9 General purpose bombs capable of being carried by the A-10 include the 500 pound class MK-36 Destructor, MK-82 Low Drag General Purpose (LDGP), MK-82 Snakeye (SE), MK-82 AIR (BSU-49/B), BDU-50 inert practice bomb; and the 1,000 pound class MK-84 LDGP. Though not capable of lasing targets, the A-10 can carry GBU-10 1,000 pound laser guided bombs and GBU-12 500 pound laser guided bomb.

MK-20 Rockeye cluster bombs can be carried in the same manner as other 500 pound class weapons both singly and on TERs. SUU-30 dispensers can also be carried both singly and on TERs on all stations except station 6. The SUU-30 is capable of being configured as the CBU-24B/B, CBU-49B/B, CBU-52B/B, CBU-58A/B, CBU-71/B, and CBU-71A/B. Both the SUU-64/B CBU-89/B Combined Effects Munitions (CEM) and the SUU-65/B CBU-87/B Gator weapons can be carried singly on all stations except station 6.

The BLU-52 chemical bombs can be carried on stations 3, 4, 5, 7, 8, and 9.

Miscellaneous Stores and Auxiliary Fuel Tanks

The SUU-25 20mm Vulcan gun pod can be carried on stations 5 and 7. MXU-648/A cargo pods can be carried on stations 3, 4, 6, 8, and 9. Jettisonable 600 gallon external fuel tanks manufactured by Royal Industries or Sargent Fletcher can be carried on stations 4, 6, and 8.

MXU-648 CARGO PODS

CHARACTERISTICS

LENGTH	10 FT 10 IN.
DIAMETER	19 IN.
DOOR SIZE	12 X 22.6 inches

A-10 PAINT SCHEMES

A-10 paint schemes have evolved over the past twenty plus years of U.S. Air Force service. camouflage development. Including preproduction, the A-10 has carried at least fifteen different color schemes, twelve in preproduction and operational testing, with three additional schemes seeing operational use.

YA-10A

The two YA-10 prototypes were delivered in overall gloss Aircraft Gray 16473, the Air Force standard exterior finish. Camouflage was first applied for the 1974 flyoff against the A-7. Rather than using the USAF tactical aircraft standard Southeast Asia camouflage, an new gray paint the Air Force had developed for use on AC-130 gunships, FS 36118 Gunship Gray, was applied to the second prototype. This "gunship quality" paint had been developed to improve defense against optical, IR, and radar-guided weapons.

PREPRODUCTION AIRCRAFT

Concerned with the A-10s primary threat, ground fire, the Air Force stressed celestial camouflages, that is those which would camouflage the aircraft against a sky background. Each of the six preproduction airframes was delivered in a different scheme.

Aircraft 73-1664 was painted overall 36118 Gunship Gray.

Aircraft 73-1665 was painted in a mottled gray using an uneven overspray of white over a black base coat.

Aircraft 73-1666 wore overall 36320 Dark Ghost Gray.

Aircraft 73-1667 wore a special new Honeywell paint called "40% Reflecting MASK-10A." (MASK-10A paints had no FS595 equivalents, and colors shifted with lighting conditions.)

73-1668 and 73-1669 had mottled white patterns over a black base coat.

73-1667 had a special paint mix whose colors would shift between light gray and a pea soup green depending on the light conditions. (Don Logan)

CHAPTER 3: A-10 DESCRIPTION

OPERATIONAL TEST PAINT SCHEMES

By the time the A-10 went into production an official scheme had not been selected. There is some disagreement over the first five production airframes.

The first three production aircraft (75-0258, 75-0259, and 75-0260) were painted an overall FS36375 Light Ghost Gray. The next two aircraft (75-0261 and 75-0262) schemes combined a MASK-10A with a Ghost Gray. 75-0261 was painted with dark Ghost Gray FS 36320 on upper surfaces and sides, and light MASK-10A on undersides. 75-0262 was painted in reverse with MASK-10A on uppers and sides and 36320 Dark Ghost Gray below.

The first production camouflage, though only used on fourteen aircraft, was first applied to 75-0263. The paints were DeSoto versions of MASK-10A (called "Super DesothanF") in 30% (darker) and 50% (lighter) reflectance values. The pattern had asymmetrical dark patches on both sides of the forward fuselage

During an operational testing at Nellis, it was determined that while tactics could help the A-10s evade ground defenses, the bright MASK-10A celestial colors made the A-10 a target easily located from above by defending fighters. Under the Joint Attack Weapons System (JAWS) evaluation terrestrial camouflages (that is those camouflages designed to hide the aircraft against a ground background) would be tested. The resulting camouflages have been called the JAWS Schemes. Only four aircraft (75-0258, 75-0259, 75-0260, and 75-0262) were painted in variations of the JAWS Schemes. One color was used as a base, with up to four other colors spotted on from spray cans and brushes. The colors primarily used were FS36231 gray, FS34092 dark green, FS30118 brown, FS34102 olive green, and FS30227 tan. While the aircraft participating in JAWS and JAWS II proved that terrestrial camouflages could be effective, they also proved the small spots did not improve the camouflage effectiveness, and created a maintenance nightmare, since touch-ups required the stocking all of the different paint colors used in the camouflage.

TAC development of an improved terrestrial camouflage. A single color scheme of FS34092 dark green, FS34102 medium green, or FS36231 Dark Gull Gray was recommended. TAC decided to apply a pattern of all three colors, and in September, 1978 aircraft 75-0266 and 75-0269 were repainted in the new scheme. FS36118 was substituted for FS36231 and applied to 75-0259. In the production European I scheme, FS36081, an even darker gray, was substituted for FS36118.

With European I adopted as the standard, all A-10s wore one of the European I patterns. During Desert Shield, it became apparent that dark green was not effectively color for a terrestrial camouflage flying above the desert. The 917th TFW, AFRES, at Barksdale AFB developed two test camouflages - a gray called Flipper and a sand-and-brown called Peanut. 76-0552 was painted in Peanut, and 76-0530, 77-0205, 77-0227, 77-0268, 77-0269, and 77-0272 were reported painted in the Flipper scheme. The Air Force did not approve of these schemes and the jets scheduled for deployment to the Persian Gulf were repainted back to European I. An A-10 of the 10th TFW at RAF Alconbury was reported to have been repainted in a monochromatic gray, but it too was repainted immediately.

75-0261's pain scheme used MASK-10A paint with dark ghost gray (FS36320) on the upper surfaces and light MASK-10A on the lower surfaces. (Don Logan)

A-10 PAINT SCHEMES

75-0263 was the first of 14 aircraft to be painted in the A-10's first production camouflage. (Mick Roth)

75-0265 was one of the aircraft with the early camouflage with dark gray top and sides and light gray bottom. (Mick Roth)

CHAPTER 3: A-10 DESCRIPTION

OPERATIONAL PAINT SCHEMES

The second production scheme, but the first to be painted on A-10s in any appreciable number (146 aircraft) was the False Canopy Scheme, also using DeSoto's 30% and 50% MASK-10A. The paint was reformulated to alleviate weathering problems, causing the colors to become slightly greener. The pattern was completely revised, with darker upper surfaces and sides, and lighter under surfaces and shadow areas. A FS 36118 Gunship Gray false canopy was added on the underside below the cockpit.

The factory delivered its first European I aircraft in January, 1979. The camouflage scheme was made up of FS34092 dark green, FS34102 medium green, or FS36081 Dark Gray. With European I as the official camouflage for the A-10, depots and unit paint shops began re-painting earlier aircraft in the European I scheme.

During the late 1980s several OA-10s of the 51st TFW at Osan AB, South Korea, were painted overall FS36118 Gunship Gray. They were later repainted in standard European I colors.

After Desert Storm, the A-10's were repainted in a camouflage similar to the pre-European I camouflage. The False Canopy Scheme was used as the pattern. Light Ghost Gray (FS36375) and Dark Ghost Gray (FS36320) replaced the MASK-10A paints. All the A-10s are presently being repainted in the two tone ghost gray scheme.

A-10 PAINT SCHEMES

79-0104, City Of Westfield is seen here painted in standard European I camouflage. (Tom Kaminski)

79-0174 is seen here in the new scheme which uses light and dark ghost gray. (Don Logan)

CHAPTER 3: A-10 DESCRIPTION

EUROPEAN I PAINT SCHEME

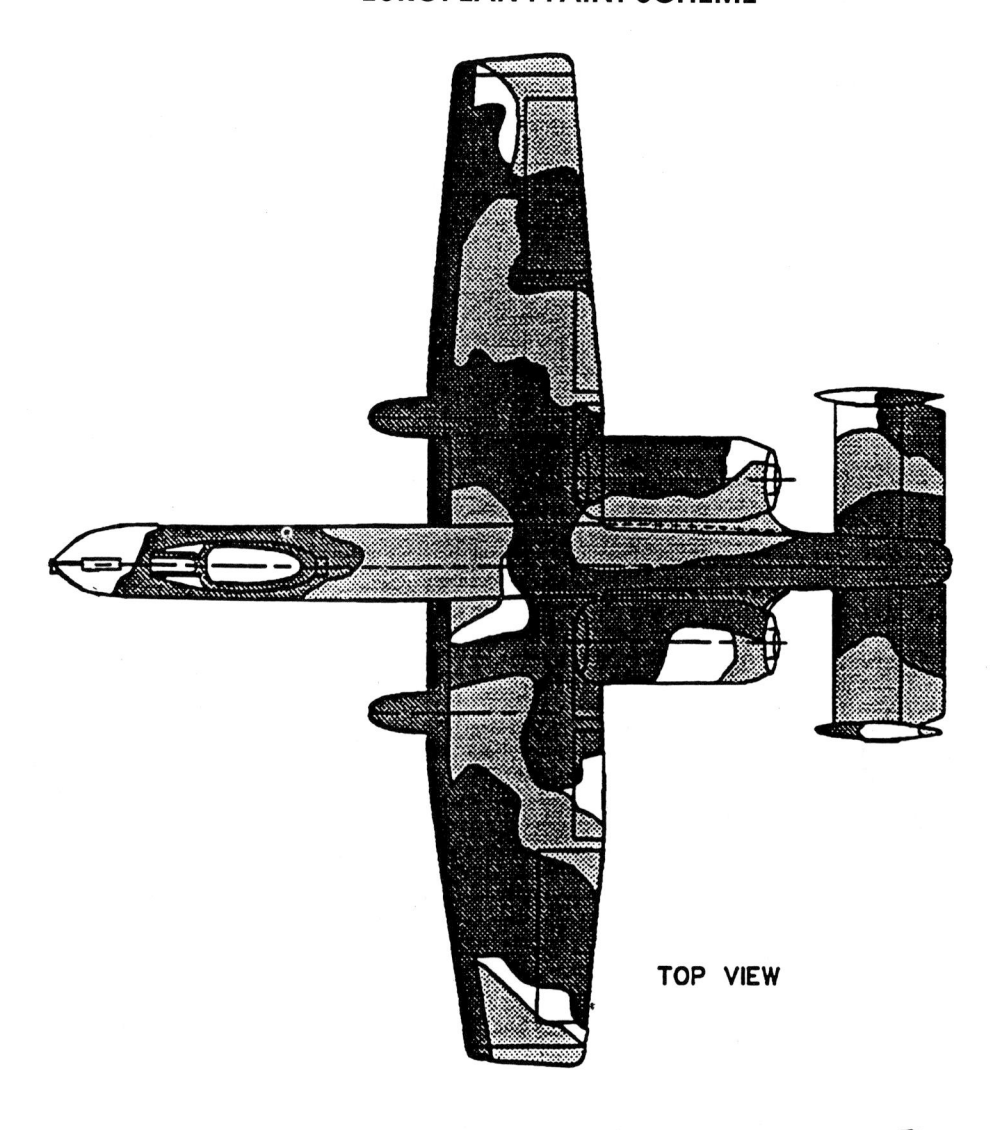

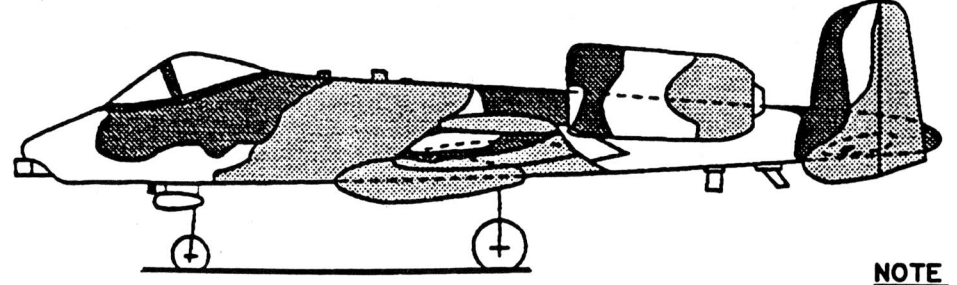

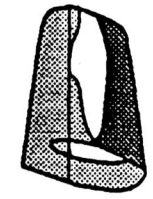

TOP VIEW

L.H. SIDE VIEW

INSIDE LEFT VERTICAL STAB

☐ COLOR NO. 36081 DARK GRAY (GUNSHIP QUALITY)
▒ COLOR NO. 34102 LIGHT GREEN (GUNSHIP QUALITY)
▓ COLOR NO. 34092 DARK GREEN (GUNSHIP QUALITY)

NOTE
GUNSHIP QUALITY BLACK, COLOR NO. 37038 MIL-C-83286, IS USED FOR ALL INSIGNIA AND MARKINGS. BOTH RUDDERS SHALL BE COMPLETELY PAINTED COLOR NO. 34102 LIGHT GREEN (GUNSHIP QUALITY) WITH NO OVERSPRAY OF OTHER COLORS.

A-10 PAINT SCHEMES

EUROPEAN I PAINT SCHEME

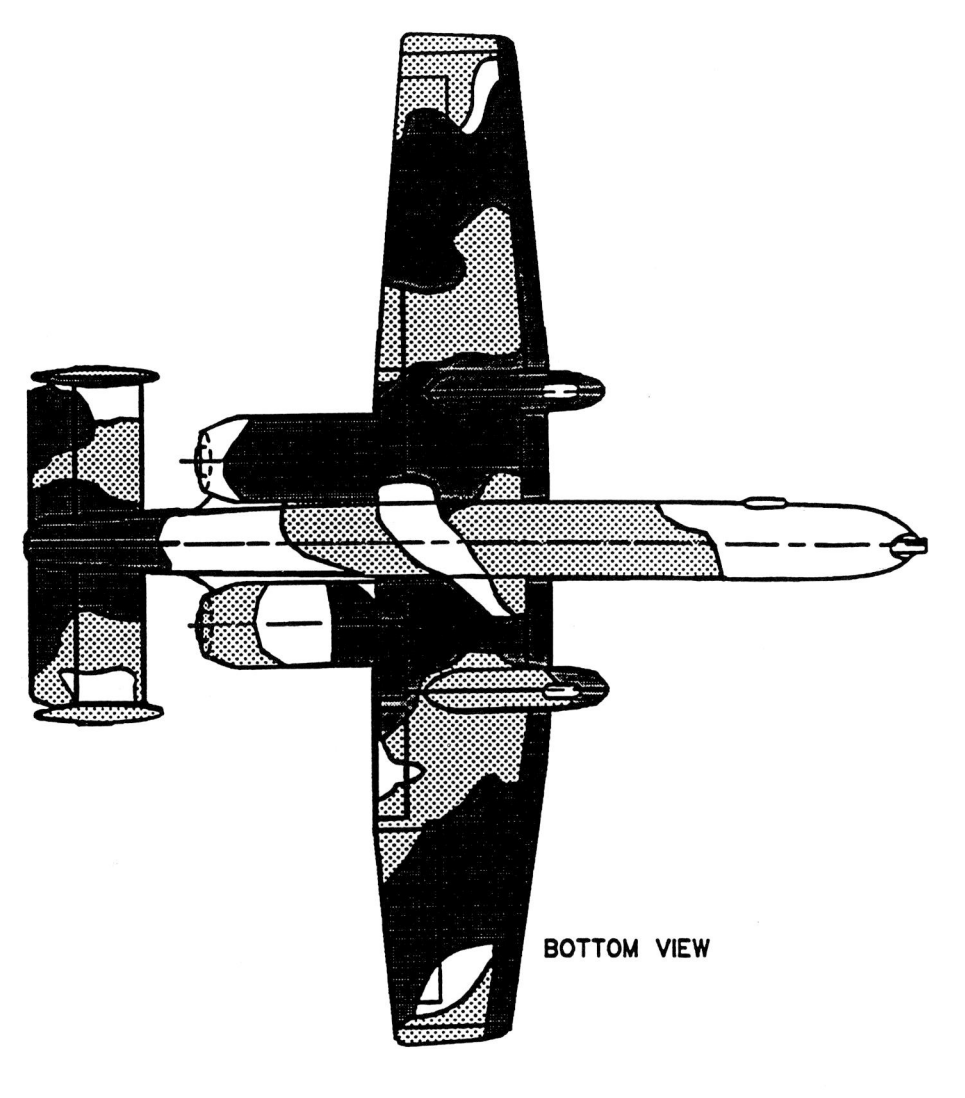

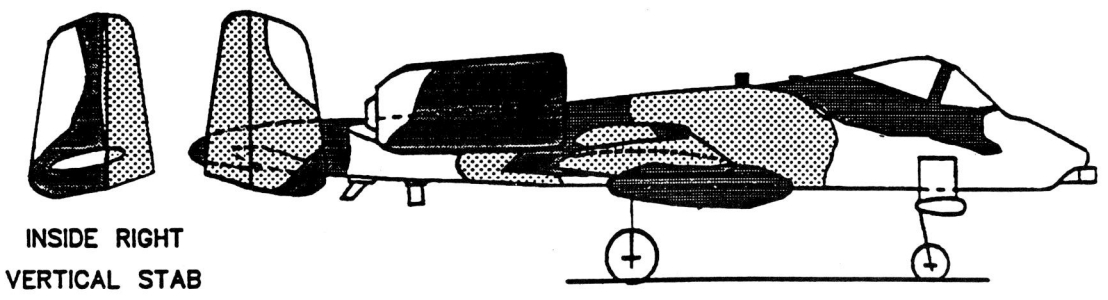

BOTTOM VIEW

INSIDE RIGHT
VERTICAL STAB

R.H. SIDE VIEW

CHAPTER 3: A-10 DESCRIPTION

GHOST GRAY PAINT SCHEME

TOP VIEW

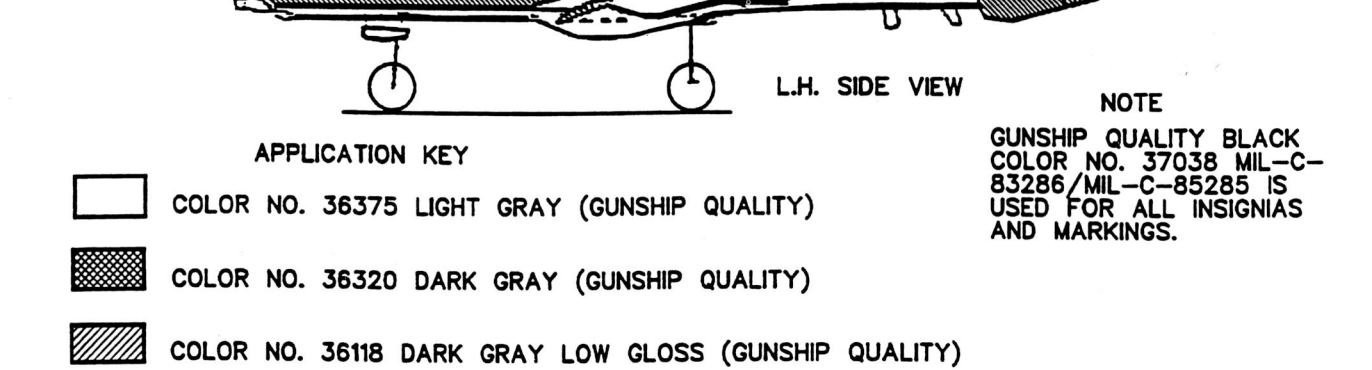

L.H. SIDE VIEW

APPLICATION KEY

- COLOR NO. 36375 LIGHT GRAY (GUNSHIP QUALITY)
- COLOR NO. 36320 DARK GRAY (GUNSHIP QUALITY)
- COLOR NO. 36118 DARK GRAY LOW GLOSS (GUNSHIP QUALITY)

NOTE

GUNSHIP QUALITY BLACK COLOR NO. 37038 MIL-C-83286/MIL-C-85285 IS USED FOR ALL INSIGNIAS AND MARKINGS.

A-10 PAINT SCHEMES

GHOST GRAY PAINT SCHEME

BOTTOM VIEW

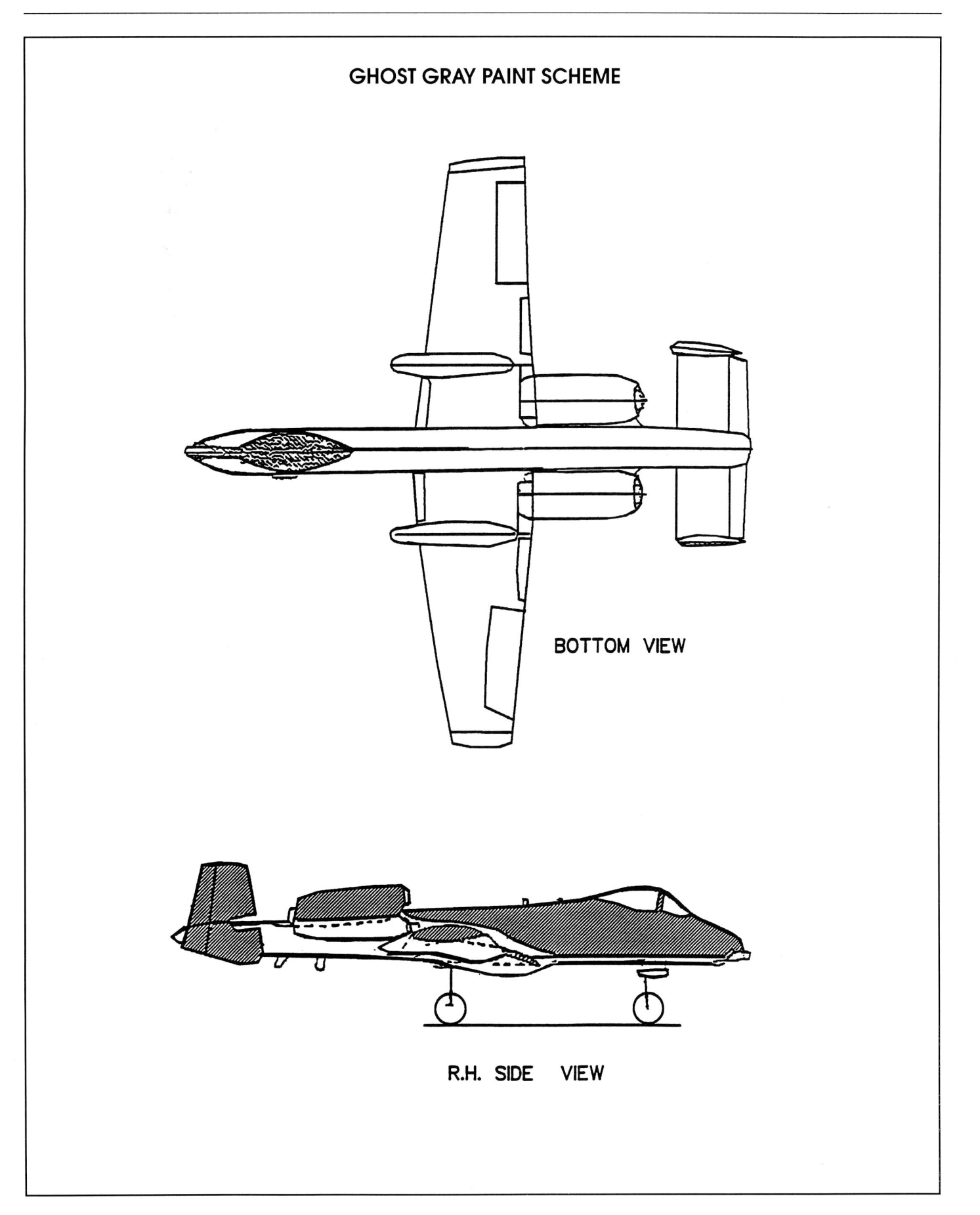

R.H. SIDE VIEW

CHAPTER 3: A-10 DESCRIPTION

TAIL NUMBERS/CODES

Early A-10A serial number presentation on the tail was a line of six-inch black digits applied four feet below the base of the fin cap. The number was last five digits of the serial number, excluding the first digit of the contract year. Zeros were added if necessary, so 75-0258 used 50258 on the tail while 73-1664 used 31664.

In the mid 1970s Davis-Monthan applied oversized TAC style tail code and serial number presentation on the first three 1975 year aircraft (75-0259, 75-0260 and 75-0261).

The A-10 now use the standard tail code presentation made up of the two letter unit identifier in 12" letters and the aircraft serial number below the tail code The serial number is made up "AF" in 2 1/2 letters on top of two 2 1/2 inch digits, normally corresponding to the fiscal year in which the aircraft was procured, painted below the "AF." The last three digits in 6 inch numbers follow the year block. Using the examples in the first paragraph, 75-0258 would simply use 258 after the year block. 73-1664 would drop the 1 and use 664 with the year block.

Commanders or Flagship aircraft modify this convention and used highlighted tail codes and highlighted numbers to display the unit number. If possible aircraft with the unit number in their serial number are used. For example 80-0212 is used as the 12th Air Force flagship and 77-0222 was used as the 22nd TASTS flagship.

The last three of the serial are usually repeated side of the wheel well pod or on the nose. If duplicates of the last three digits occur (as in 79-0240 and 80-0240) a four digit number is made by adding the last digit of the fiscal year. For example 79-0240 would be 9240 and 80-0240 would remain 240. Some units repeated the serial number above the refueling receptacle for identification during communications out inflight refuelings.

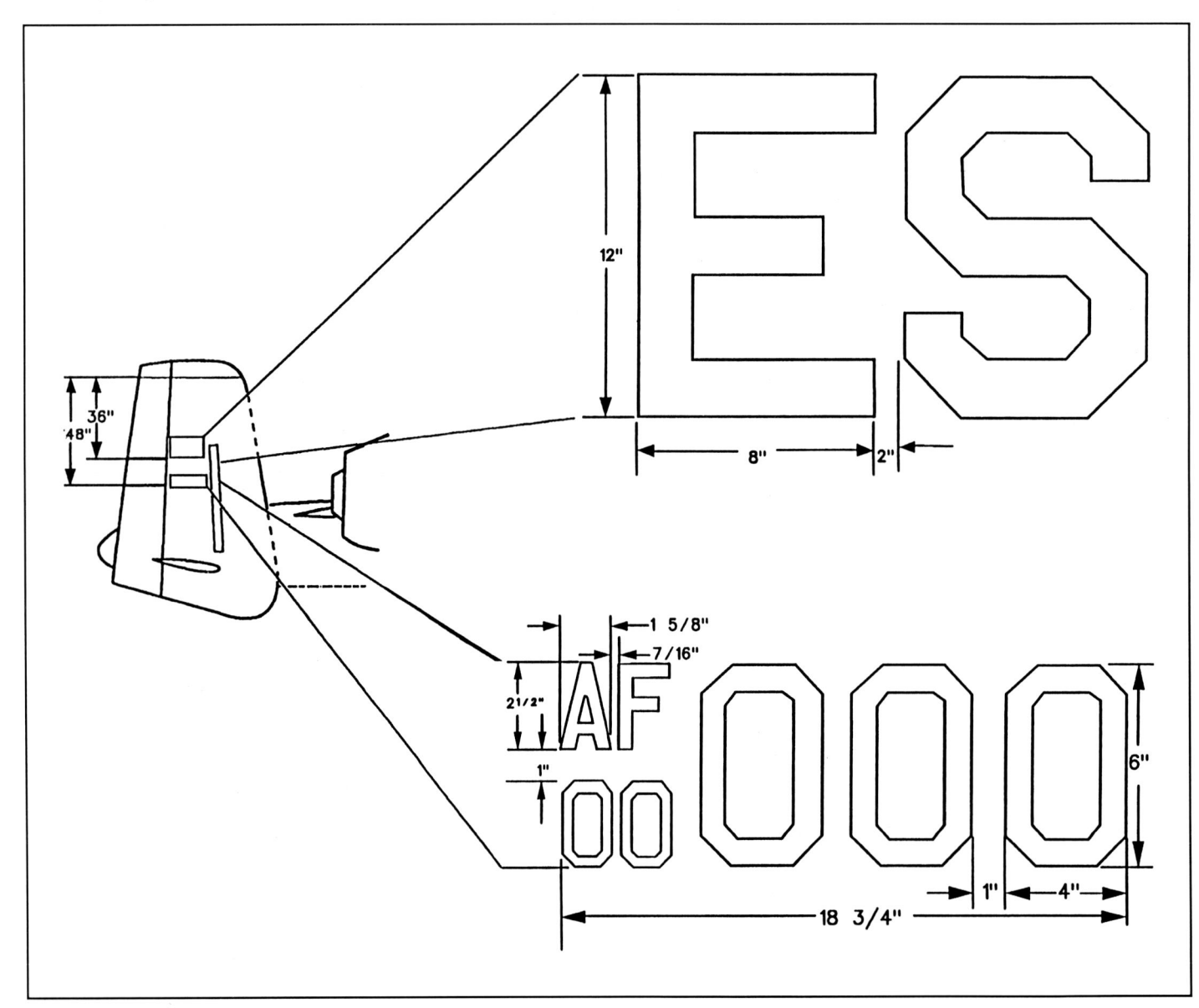

230

TAIL NUMBERS/CODES

75-0261, when photographed at DM AFB on March 29, 1976 was wearing the oversized tail code and serial numbers which the 354th TFW used on their first few aircraft. (Ray Leader)

75-0276 wore small tail codes and the early serial number presentation when photographed at DM AFB on June 1, 1977. (Ben Knowles)

CHAPTER 3: A-10 DESCRIPTION

This view of 79-0135 while assigned to the 23rd wing, shows the serial number applied above the air refueling receptacle. (Don Logan)

TURNING RADIUS AND GROUND CLEARANCE

- 31'-5" / 23'-0"
- 34'-6" / 22'-2"
- 43'-5" / 5'-9"
- PIVOT POINT
- L/H MAIN GEAR RADIUS
- R/H MAIN GEAR RADIUS
- NOSE GEAR RADIUS
- GUN MUZZLE RADIUS
- VERTICAL STABILIZER RADIUS
- WING TIP RADIUS
- 46'-0"
- 50'-0" RUNWAY WIDTH
- 2'-0"

GROUND CLEARANCE

- 5'-0"
- 9'-1"
- 5'-0"
- 14'-8"

CHAPTER 3: A-10 DESCRIPTION

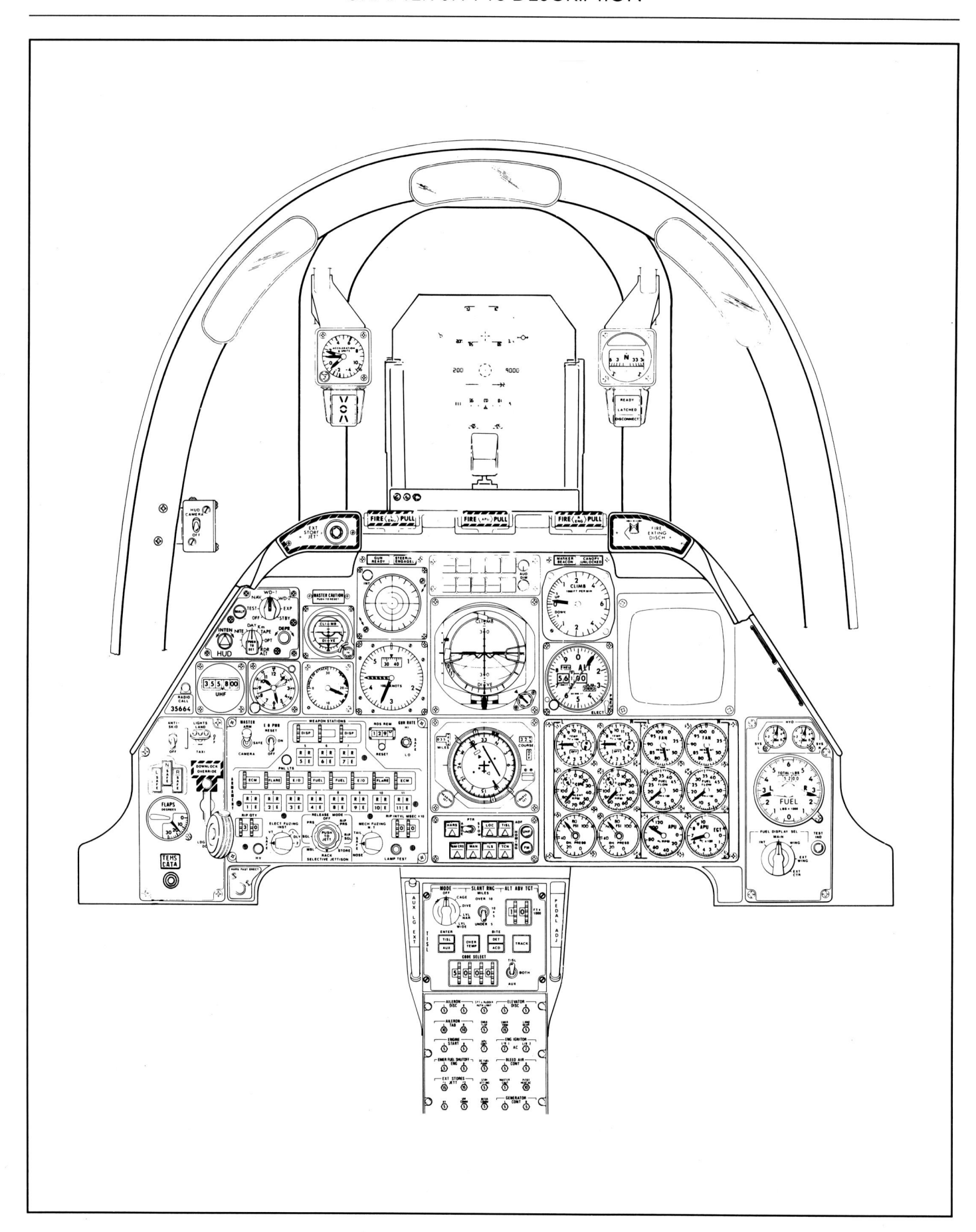

INSTRUMENT PANELS

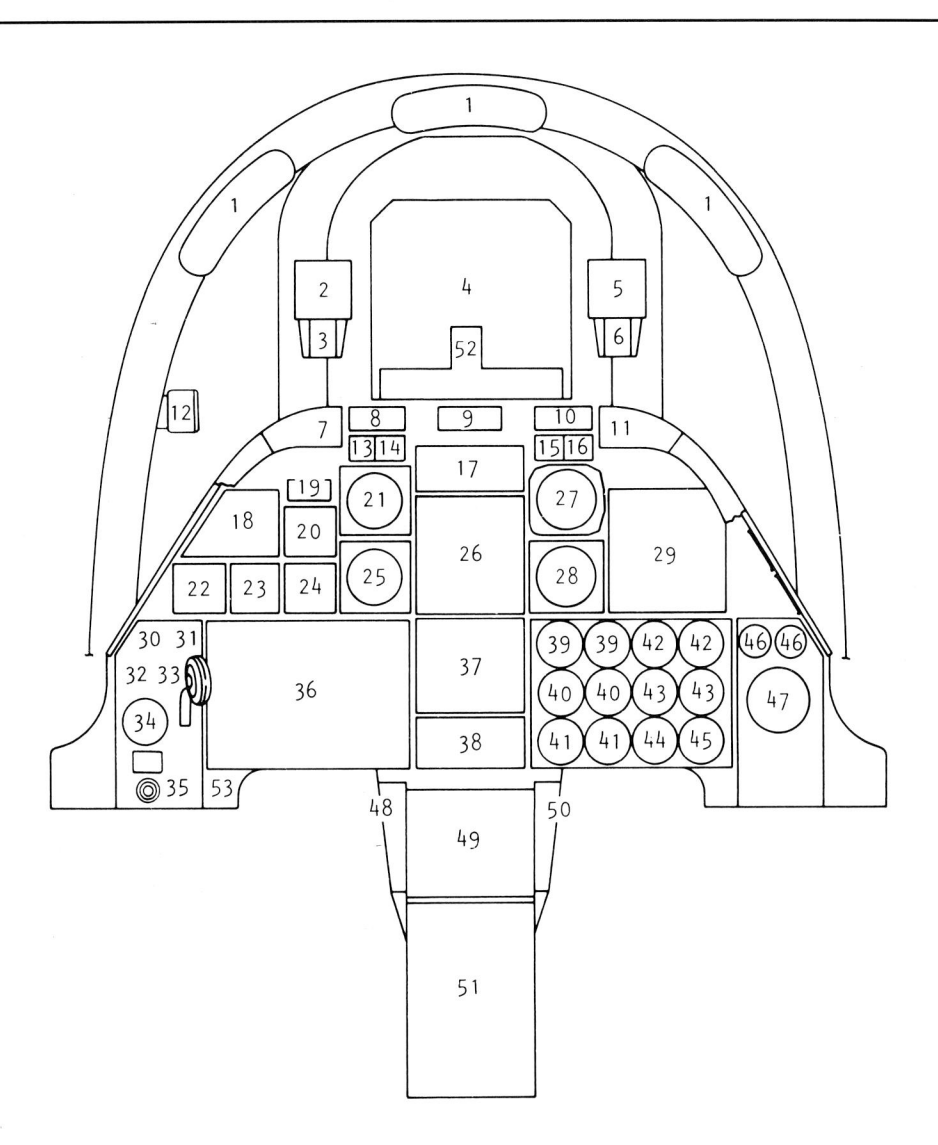

INSTRUMENT PANEL (TYPICAL)

1. Rear View Mirrors
2. Accelerometer
3. Angle of Attack indexers
4. Head Up Display (HUD)
5. Standby Compass
6. Air Refuel Status Lights
7. External Stores Jettison Switch
8. Left Engine Fire Pull Handle
9. APU Fire Pull Handle
10. Right Engine Fire Pull Handle
11. Fire Extinguishing Agent Discharge Switch
12. Gun Camera Switch
13. Gun Ready Light
14. NoseWheel Steering Engaged Light
15. Marker Beacon Light
16. Canopy Unlocked Light
17. RHAW Control Indicator
18. HUD Control Panel
19. Master Caution Light
20. Standby Attitude Indicator
21. RHAW Azimuth Indicator
22. UHF Remote Chan/Freq Indicator
23. Clock
24. Angle of Attack Indicator
25. Airspeed Indicator
26. Attitude Director Indicator (ADI)
27. Vertical Velocity Indicator
28. Altimeter
29. TV Monitor
30. Anti-Skid Switch
31. Landing/Taxi Lights Switch
32. Landing Gear Position Display
33. Landing Gear Handle and Override Button
34. Flap Position Indicator
35. TEMS Data Switch
36. Armament Control Panel
37. Horizontal Situation Indicator (HSI)
38. Navigation Mode Select Panel
39. Interstage Turbine Temperature Indicator (L & R)
40. Engine Core Speed Indicator (L & R)
41. Engine Oil Pressure Indicator (L & R)
42. Fan Speed Indicator (L & R)
43. Fuel Flow Indicator
44. APU Tachometer
45. APU Temperature Indicator
46. Hydraulic Pressure Gauge (Left Sys & Right Sys)
47. Fuel Quantity Indicator
48. Auxiliary Landing Gear Extension Handle
49. Laser Spot Seeker Panel
50. Rudder Pedal Adjustment Handle
51. Essential Circuit Breaker Panel
52. Gun Camera CTVS
53. HARS Fast Erect Switch

CHAPTER 3: A-10 DESCRIPTION

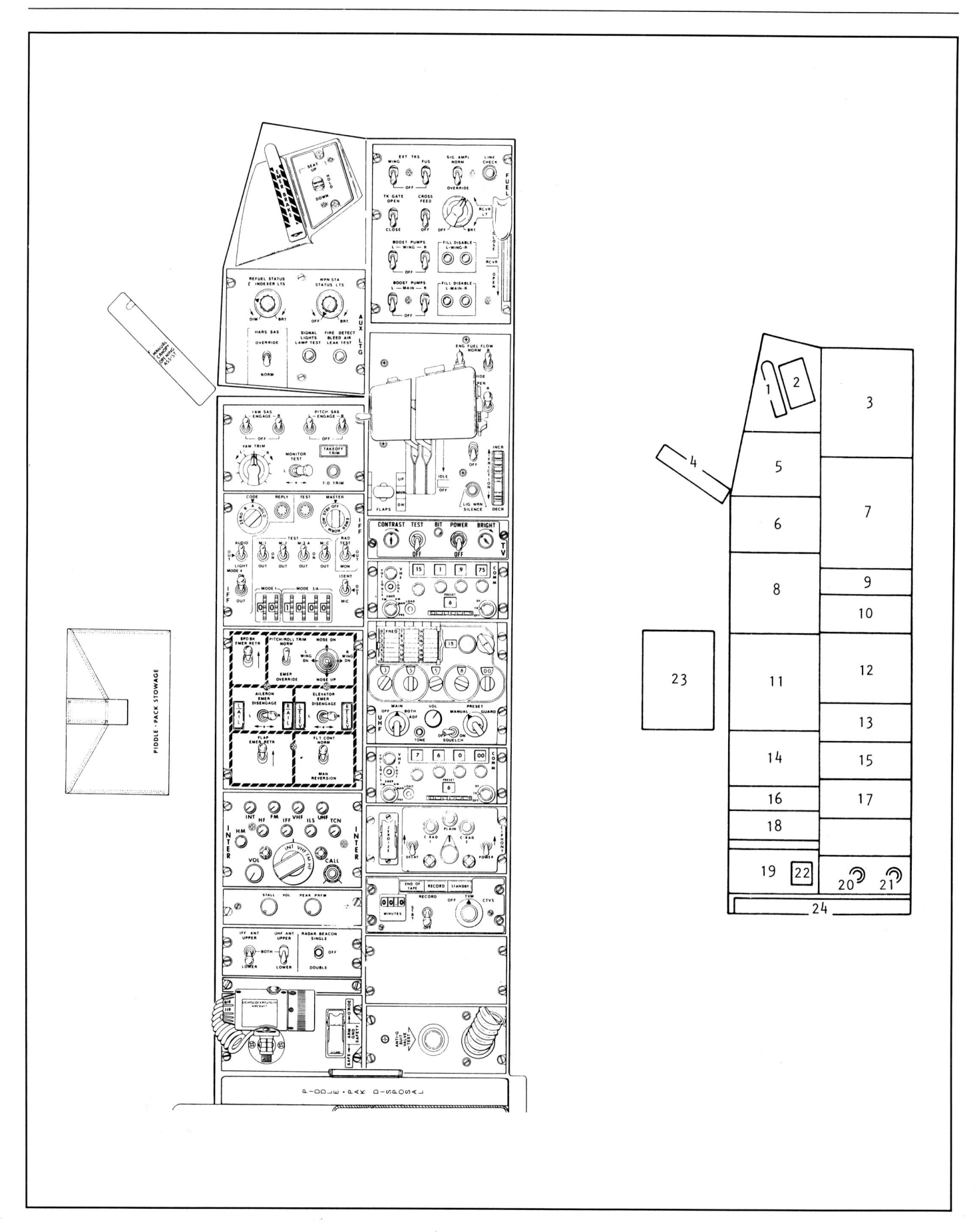

236

INSTRUMENT PANELS

**LEFT CONSOLE
(TYPICAL)**

1. Emergency Brake Handle
2. Seat Height Adjustment Switch
3. Fuel System Control Panel
4. Manual Canopy Opening Assist Handle
5. Auxiliary Lighting Control Panel
6. Stability Augmentation System Panel (SAS)
7. Throttle Quadrant
8. IFF Control Panel
9. TV Monitor Control Panel
10. VHF/AM Radio Control Panel
11. Emergency Flight Control Panel
12. UHF Radio Control Panel
13. VHF/FM Radio Control Panel
14. Intercom Control Panel
15. C I PHONY Panel
16. Stall Warning Control Panel
17. CTVS/AVTR Control Panel
18. Antenna Select Panel
19. Utility Light
20. Anti-G Suit Valve Test Button
21. Anti-G Suit Hose
22. Armament Override Switch
23. Piddle Pak Stowage
24. Piddle Pak Disposal

CHAPTER 3: A-10 DESCRIPTION

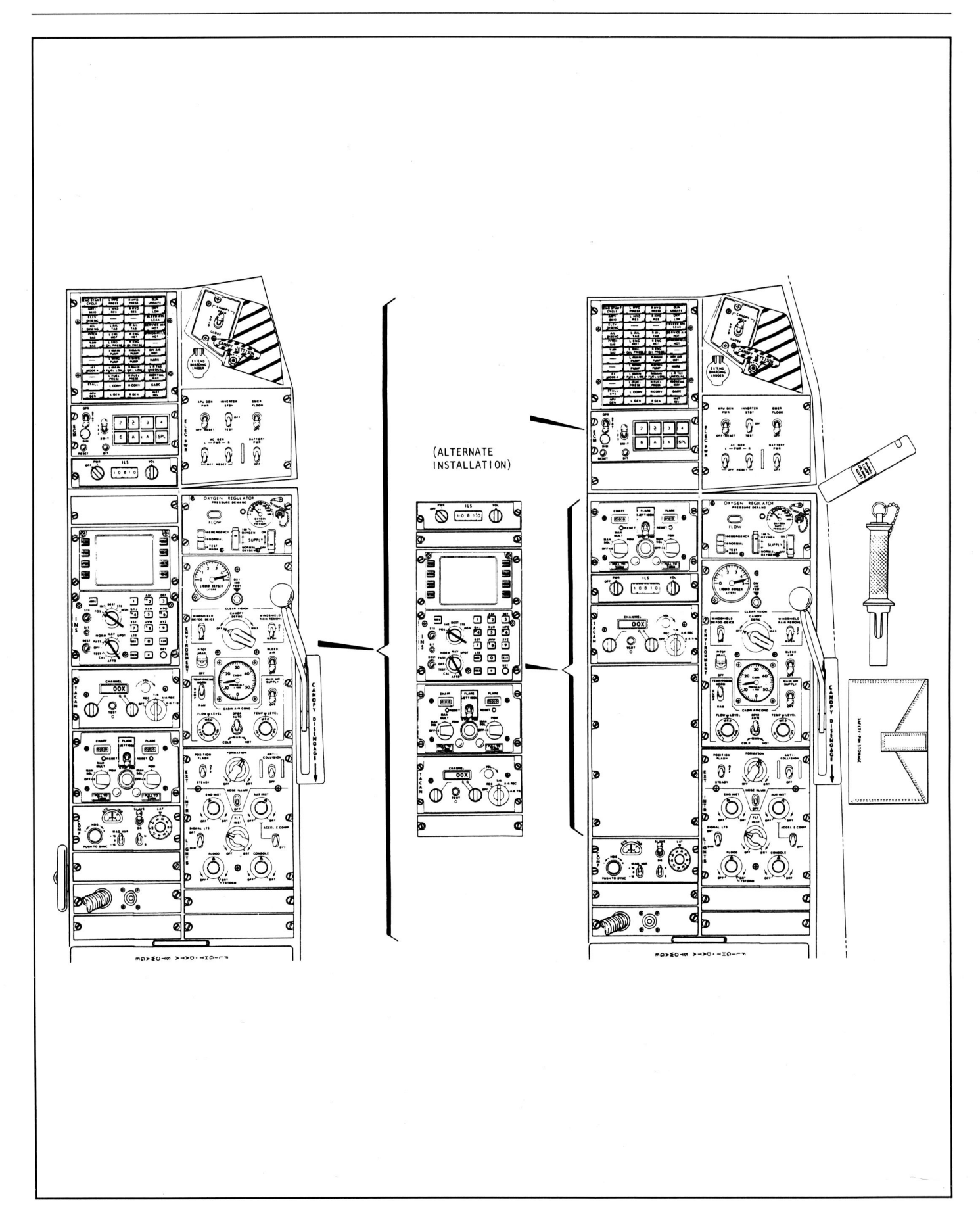

(ALTERNATE INSTALLATION)

INSTRUMENT PANELS

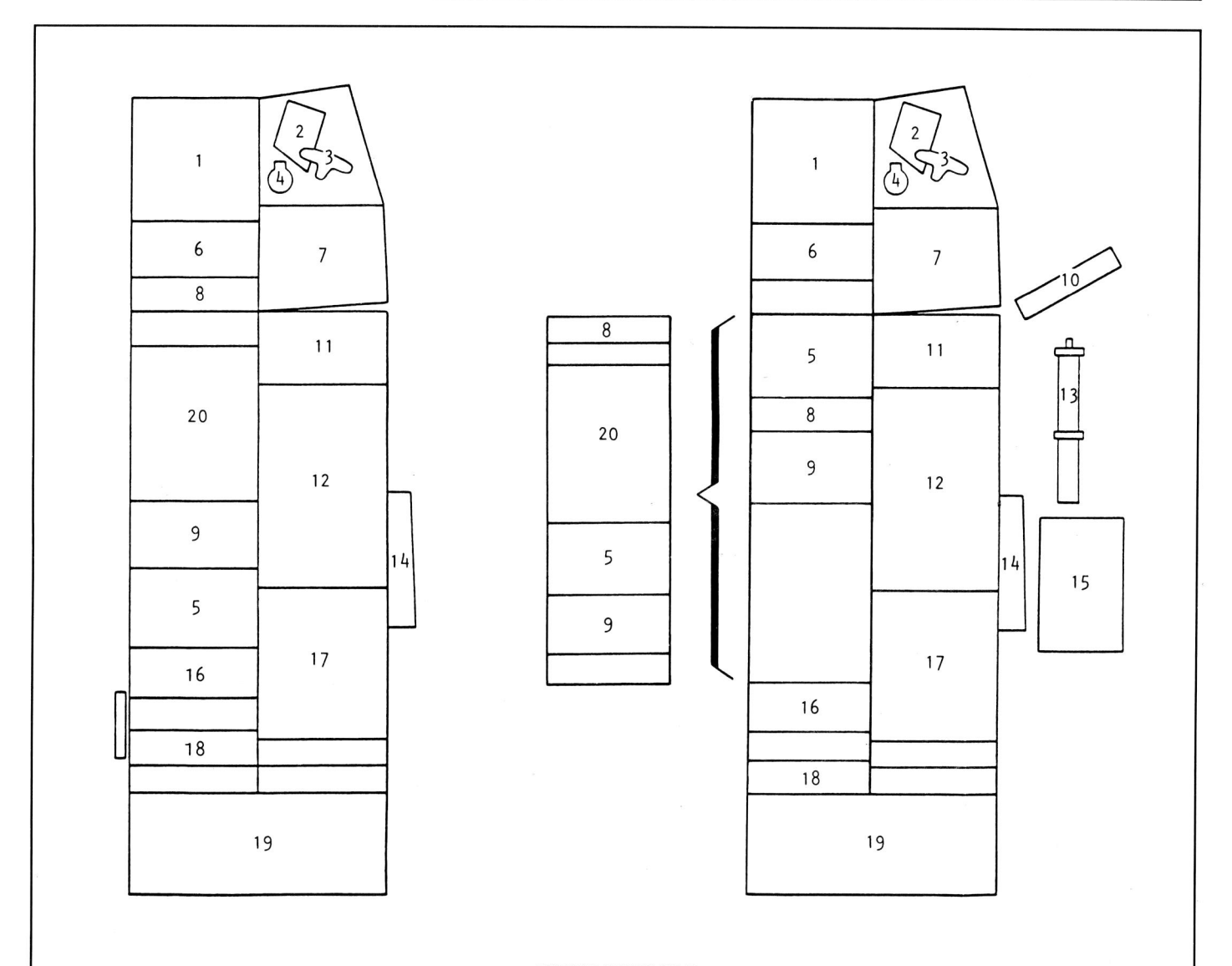

**RIGHT CONSOLE
(TYPICAL)**

1. Caution Light Panel
2. Canopy Control Switch
3. Canopy Jettison Handle
4. Boarding Ladder Extension Button
5. Chaff/Flare Control Panel
6. ECM Panel
7. Electrical Power Panel
8. ILS Control Panel
9. TACAN Control Panel
10. Manual Canopy Opening Assist Handle
11. Oxygen Control Panel
12. Environment Control Panel
13. Canopy Breaker Tool
14. Canopy Actuator Disengage Lever
15. Safety Pin Stowage
16. HARS Control Panel
17. Lighting Control Panel
18. Oxygen Hose and Intercom Connection
19. Flight Data Stowage
20. Control Display Unit (CDU)

Also from the Publisher

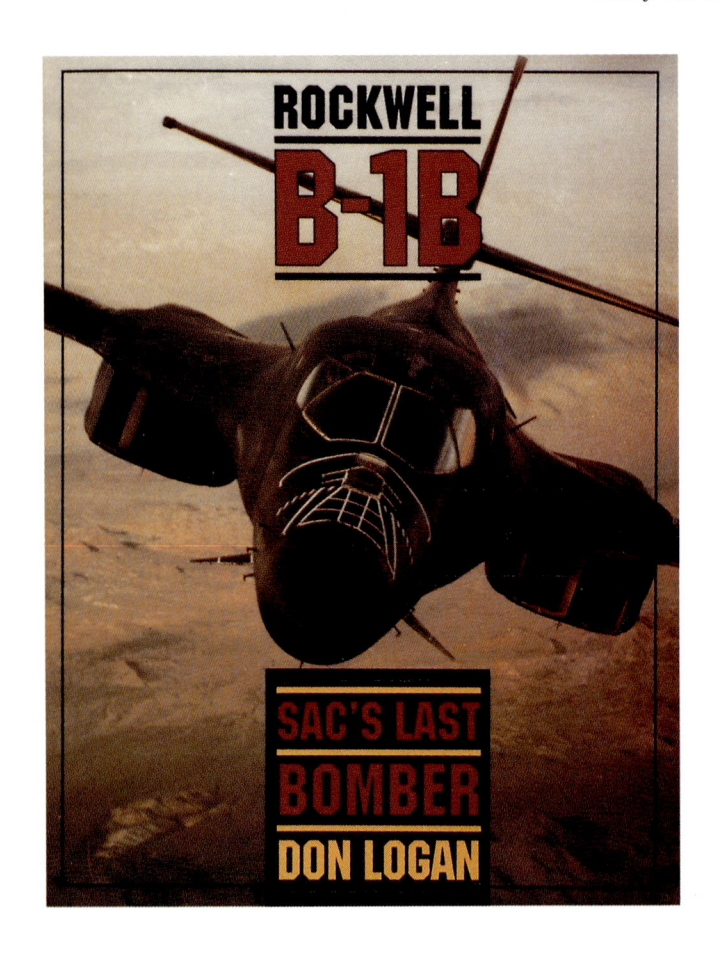

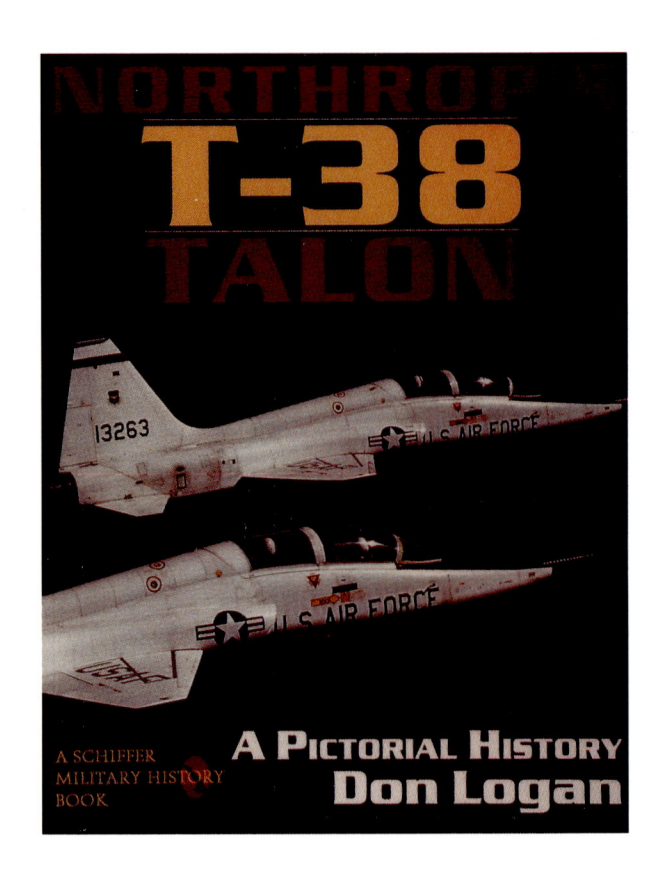

ROCKWELL B-1B
SAC's LAST BOMBER

Don Logan

Size: 8 1/2" x 11" over 400 color & b/w photos
256 pages, hard cover
ISBN: 0-88740-666-1 $49.95

NORTHROP'S T-38 TALON
A PICTORIAL HISTORY

Don Logan

Size: 8 1/2" x 11" over 300 color photographs
152 pages, soft cover
ISBN: 0-88740-800-1 $24.95

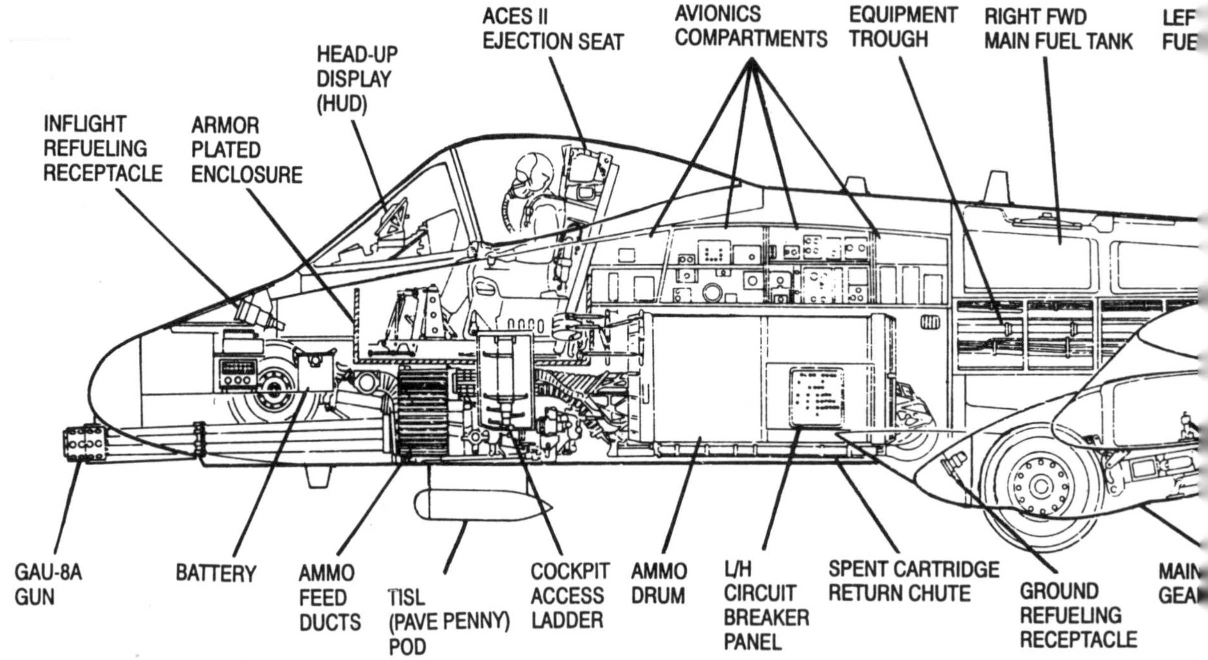
ACES II
EJECTION SEAT
AVIONICS
COMPARTMENTS
EQUIPMENT
TROUGH
RIGHT FWD
MAIN FUEL TANK
HEAD-UP
DISPLAY
(HUD)
INFLIGHT
REFUELING
RECEPTACLE
ARMOR
PLATED
ENCLOSURE
GAU-8A
GUN
BATTERY
AMMO
FEED
DUCTS
TISL
(PAVE PENNY)
POD
COCKPIT
ACCESS
LADDER
AMMO
DRUM
L/H
CIRCUIT
BREAKER
PANEL
SPENT CARTRIDGE
RETURN CHUTE
GROUND
REFUELING
RECEPTACLE

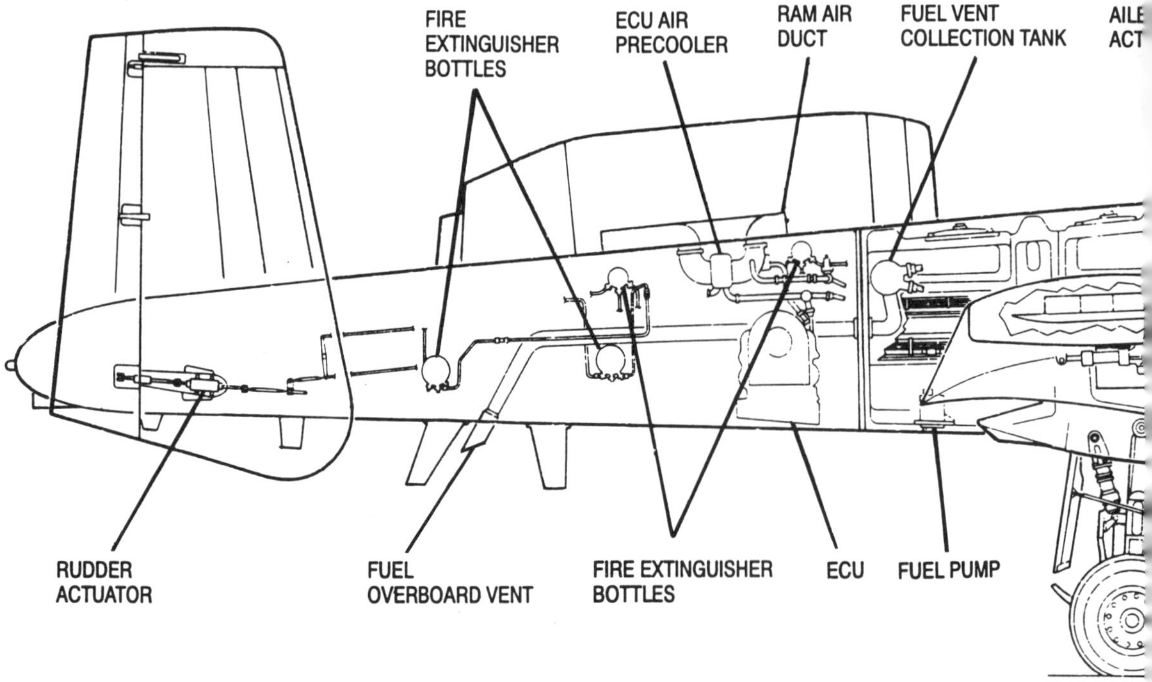
FIRE
EXTINGUISHER
BOTTLES
ECU AIR
PRECOOLER
RAM AIR
DUCT
FUEL VENT
COLLECTION TANK
RUDDER
ACTUATOR
FUEL
OVERBOARD VENT
FIRE EXTINGUISHER
BOTTLES
ECU
FUEL PUMP